Offshore Outsourcing

Path to New Efficiencies in IT and Business Processes

By

Dr. Nandu Thondavadi & George Albert

ISBN: 1-4140-5513-7 (e-book)
ISBN: 1-4140-5514-5 (Paperback)
ISBN: 1-4140-5515-3 (Dust Jacket)

This book is printed on acid free paper.

1stBooks - rev. 05/20/04

Acknowledgments

Many people have helped and educated us in the making of this book. The topic is so dynamic and the focus kept changing continually that we never felt the book was complete and will always be "work in progress".

To acknowledge is a formality, but never in the case of deep indebtedness. Scott Bayman and Pramod Bhasin, both from GE India, crystallized our thoughts into an organized format. For that we are deeply grateful. Without serious dialogue with Guillermo Wille and Alan Kocsi of GE, this book would have been just an academic exercise. Throughout the project, we were blessed with insights from many people in the industry. Meera Sanyal of ABN-AMRO Bank educated us on captive business process outsourcing. Efrain Jovel, who retired from Citibank - Latin American Consumer Banking operations, provided us with first-hand insights on IT operations consolidation and the "onboarding" process of offshore vendors. We thank Narayana Murthy of Infosys Technologies for allowing us to feature his global delivery model for outsourcing and facilitating extensive dialogue with management of their BPO unit, Progeon.

We have been blessed by having many good friends with whom we could chew over different ideas that may have gone into this work. We thank Rohit Rao of Ad Factors, Sudarshan Narasimhamurthy of Infosys, and Subrat Mohanty of Progeon.

We would be remiss, though, if we did not thank Elaine Freedman for her superlative edits of the manuscript.

And finally, we thank Mascon for its sponsorship of the book.

Our families stood behind us during this project while we spent weekends and holidays researching for the project and agonizing whether this work is even worth pursuing. We thank our spouses, Paru Thondavadi and Anu George. Our children, Natasha Thondavadi and Neal George, were always a boundless source of inspiration.

Table of Contents

Preface

Stripped of jargon, offshore outsourcing is nothing but the cross-border re-allocation of labor. It is the manifestation of Adam Smith's classic economic theory on a wider scale. Like all value principles, the essence of division of labor does not change when its scope of application broadens. Smith's theory states that labor resources are best used when work tasks are divided among different workers to enable specialization. Division of labor is so basic to economic activity that its importance is often overlooked in the real world. This specialization makes for foreign trade, where countries produce goods and services that they excel in and later exchange with other countries for goods and services they cannot produce at competitively affordable costs.

Offshore outsourcing of software development and business processes is division of labor in action. Businesses seeking specialized and cost-effective labor move to countries that satisfy their needs. I have experienced it at GE, a pioneer in low-cost country outsourcing. GE helped create the Indian software industry when it contracted a significant percentage of its development work to four key Indian suppliers. We targeted 70 percent of all software work to be outsourced, and 70 percent of what was outsourced to be with one of the four Indian firms. Finally, we targeted 70 percent of this work to be actually done in India. GE's success with this strategy provided credibility and proof that India could deliver to the highest of quality standards. Following our success with software, we went after business processes and again helped create a new industry.

This book provides an in-depth look at the outsourcing process, the benefits that companies accrue, and the path to achieve them. Quoting extensively from examples of leading businesses, the book draws crucial lessons for both uninitiated and conversant companies. Even companies that have outsourced processes to low-cost countries can learn from the experience of others covered in this book.

The need is clear. The reasons to outsource processes offshore are many and include cost, speed, scale, and the ability to focus on the core. Offshore outsourcing fulfilled these needs for GE, as well as for Citibank, American Express, HSBC, Dell, and a host of other companies. The most forceful argument for offshore outsourcing is cost. It is the primary reason to move processes offshore. However, once a process is outsourced, the additional benefits—speed, scale, and ability to focus on core—crystallize.

Labor arbitrage can reduce cost of operating a process by almost 40 per cent. Relocating processes from high-wage countries such as the US and the UK to cost-effective knowledge domains like India reduces labor costs by as much as 70 to 80 percent. After adding the cost of setting up a new communications infrastructure and other overheads, the transactional cost saving equates to between 40 to 50 percent. The cost advantage of moving to India is nearly 25 percent for lower-valued services and as high as 60 percent for the processes higher up in the value chain. Cost savings is not a one-time affair. Process improvements and currency devaluation have increased savings over the years.

GE has forecast a savings of over $1 billion dollars by 2005. This number will be achieved by creating about 5,200 technology and software jobs and 19,000 back-office jobs in GE India. The savings also include software supplier headcount in India, which is projected to stand at 12,500 in 2005, making a total of nearly 37,000 jobs in India supporting GE globally.

These cost reductions free up money to invest in new initiatives. With outsourcing to a third party as GE does with much of its software development, capital investments can be avoided, as the supplier bears this cost. In effect, the funds available due to the cost savings can be invested in the core activities of the company. An added benefit is the ability of management to focus time on the core functions of the organization. Accounts payable, processing credit card approvals, analyzing sales and expenses, answering telephone inquiries, and a myriad of other business processes are all "back-room" activities. But for the offshore service provider, these all are "front-room," core functions. Business leaders of offshore process centers of excellence wake up thinking about what their teams must accomplish every day. It is what drives them. It is what they are measured on. It is what they are paid to do. Hence, these back-room activities of the parent corporation or business unit benefit from far more management attention than they would receive at the home location. Higher quality levels, more efficient process, and improved customer service are valuable by-products. In GE, we use Six Sigma tools to measure these improvements.

During the US economic boom of the mid and late 1990s, when hiring outstanding talent was tough and time-consuming, locating key back-room processes and call centers to India allowed GE to provide adequate contextual support. This, in turn, made it possible to grow at a much more rapid pace in key sectors such as healthcare, insurance and private label credit cards. During this same period of economic expansion, difficulty in hiring qualified talent and high attrition rates at call centers often led to poor customer service, loss of business, and slower growth.

Offshore delivery is able to scale operations quickly due to its proximity to talent. Unlike in Europe or North America, where the availability of skilled software engineers and developers is limited and where visa regulations restrict the free flow of resources, a software supplier in India can set up a facility of 300 people in less than a month, if needed. GE's business processing arm, GECIS, hired and trained college graduates at the rate of 500 to 600 a month for long periods of time. We never would have been able to add 700 scientists and engineers, many with PhDs, to our US research center in the nine months it took to bring the Welch Technology Center online in India.

Operations in India and other Asian countries enable round-the-clock software development, which adds speed to projects. Work completed in India can be downloaded at the end of the day for review in the US at the start of the day, cutting development time by a half to a third. The same round-the-clock benefits apply to business processes outsourced to Asia.

As you read through this book, you will notice several other tangential benefits of outsourcing. Today, there is no compelling reason to keep contextual processes on-site when cost-effective and superior solutions are available in lower-cost countries with highly available, highly educated, unemployed people. Getting started is not easy but, clearly, the end-game is worth the effort. Offshore outsourcing has allowed large organizations to become nimble, more cost-competitive players by shedding the burdens of back-room processes. Highly skilled software engineers are completing relatively simple tasks to highly complex solutions with difficult challenges each and every day. Engineers and scientists are developing new materials and designing new platforms and products that will be produced in locations from Shanghai to Frankfurt to San Francisco. Assured of the support from their own operations or their overseas suppliers, organizations are empowered to expand in core areas of business.

To succeed in offshore outsourcing, the push has to come from the top. In GE, Jack Welch drove the offshoring exercise, sometimes tightening budgets to push work to low-cost, developing countries. He showcased successes at leadership meetings and pressed (or at times embarrassed) other managers to follow suit—all aimed at increasing shareholder returns and making GE the most competitive company in the world. Jeff Immelt is demonstrating this same passion for low-cost country sourcing. Organizations must develop a culture that fosters outsourcing to low-cost, developing countries. GE's values—boundarylessness, speed, stretch, and diversity—helped make offshore outsourcing acceptable within the corporation. This book describes in detail what drove many companies to offshore outsourcing.

Once the organization is ready to locate operations offshore, it must make several other decisions. It must first decide if it wants to insource (own and manage the operation itself) or outsource to a third-party supplier. Next, it must identify business processes, software work, and/or technology that it wants to locate in the low-cost country. Then the company decides on the country and a supplier or suppliers, exports the process, and finally scales it. If the company elects to own and manage the operation itself, additional actions are required, including finding facilities, installing infrastructure, and hiring and training staff.

The decision to insource or outsource is usually dictated by specific requirements of the company. If the scope of outsourcing is large, and the company wants to retain functions within the organizational structure for better control, it is best to insource. That is what GE did because the scope of offshoring was very large and could benefit from the economies of scale. By the same logic, it does not make sense for small offshoring initiatives to be insourced, as overheads cannot be used to their full potential. However, if core processes like product development or R&D are exported, they tend to be captive, sometimes to protect intellectual property.

The simple rule for identifying contextual processes is to determine if the function provides a competitive edge in the marketplace. If not, it is a contextual process. This logic is similar to a fundamental covenant of strategy: Build for competitive strategy; buy for competitive parity. Contextual processes like accounting and call centers tend to be among the first to be outsourced offshore. But offshoring need not stop at back-end functions. Even core functions can be sent offshore, as Microsoft and GE do. The reason for offshoring core processes such as engineering is access to a highly educated, capable talent pool, and, by the way, lower cost.

Selecting the country for outsourcing IT and business processes is relatively simple. Businesses that need an English-speaking workforce go to India. (Ireland was an option a few years ago but is too costly today.) No other country has the number of competitively priced, highly educated, English-speaking people that India enjoys. China has strong IT skills, but language is still an issue. However, as GE is proving, China can cater to Japanese businesses. Vendor and country selection run simultaneously, and the process of selecting an offshore partner should be very rigorous. This book takes the reader through the process in detail.

Offshore outsourcing has sociopolitical implications for the US and Europe. White-collar jobs are being, and will continue to be, exported, leading to some layoffs. This is inevitable. Loss of jobs hit North America when manufacturing first relocated to Japan, then Mexico, and later China. It will happen again as services move to India and China. This is the natural progression of nations moving up the economic value chain. The transition may be painful, but the US will emerge as a stronger economic power due to the offshore outsourcing initiative. On a global level, offshore outsourcing provides two benefits. First, the US as a country will focus on core competencies, just as its individual companies will, making the country more competitive in the marketplace. Second, as the purchasing power of India and other developing countries providing offshoring services increases, they will buy more US goods. In the long run, this division of labor will be positive for world trade, as it has always proved to be in the past.

A look at China proves the point. As manufacturing shifted to China, a number of well-paying jobs were created, poverty fell, and the middle class expanded. The growing purchasing power of the Chinese proved to be a boon for the US. Its exports to China in 2002 stood at $22 billion, up from $19 billion in 2001. The 2002 US exports to China were higher than its exports to France, which clocked $19 billion, and close to its exports to Germany at $26 billion. After the initial pain, the American economy will be back in business and much higher up the value chain.

But before the US and Europe reach a new point of economic equilibrium, the road to offshoring will present hurdles. A bill moved in the New Jersey Senate that proposes to prohibit outsourcing activities of US companies will put the brakes on offshoring from the Garden State. Several other states plan to introduce similar legislation. Even though New Jersey's bill likely will fail the test of constitutional validity and standards set by the WTO, it brings into sharp focus the pain faced by US labor. Any bill of this nature is an incursion into the federal government's exclusive foreign policy domain and is irreconcilable with the federal law. The states do not have constitutional means of taking positions with foreign policy implications.

Corporations, too, will face pressure from employees to not outsource. Boeing is a case in point. After the collapse of the Soviet Union, Boeing began recruiting out-of-work Russian aerospace engineers to collaborate on space and commercial airplane projects. It opened a center in Moscow, which housed nearly 700 engineers. Seeing the growth in Moscow as a threat to their jobs, Boeing's 22,000 engineers in Seattle threatened to walk out after their contracts expired unless the Russian operations were scaled back. Even though the threat by the Seattle engineers did not force Boeing to scale back the Russian operations, it shows the pressures that outsourcing corporations can face.

Despite the hurdles, offshore outsourcing will prevail. Global competitiveness drives it; the basic laws of economics command it; and shareholder returns demand it. Companies cannot afford to miss this opportunity to cut costs, improve processes, and concentrate on core activities. Companies that refuse to outsource will carry high operating costs, thereby losing their competitive edge in the marketplace. Carrying the burden of contextual processes like accounting or call center management will make them inflexible in a rapidly changing business environment. It will also limit their abilities to expand due to the lack of capital tied up in non-core activities.

Corporations that find it difficult to accept or sell offshore outsourcing internally should look at their business as a conglomeration of business processes. Once they understand this, it will be easier to convince themselves that the contextual processes that support the core businesses can be decoupled and outsourced. Once successful, the first offshore outsourcing initiative will lead to several others until most contextual functions are sent offshore.

It can be done. We did it successfully at GE, and so have many others. The early adopters discussed in this book are reaping the benefits of offshore outsourcing. Are you on board, or will your organization continue to carry the load of costly processes in high-cost locations?

Scott Bayman
President and CEO
GE India

Introduction
The Market Space

What do General Electric, Microsoft, British Airways, Citibank, Dell, Wal-Mart, and HSBC have in common? They have all started moving operations to India and China to acquire cost-effective solutions to business processes. GE will see savings of about US $1 billion by 2005 on its call center, mortgage and insurance, accounting, and bill payment processes. Citibank saves about $75 million a year on its trade finance, check processing, customer services, loans, bills, credit cards, and cash management processes. British Airways has cut annual costs by $42 million on its passenger revenue accounting, error handling, and miles-tracking processes.

Why are EDS, Accenture, IBM Global Services, and DaimlerChrysler hiring talent in India and China? IBM Global Services plans to ramp up its 2001 staff of 2,200 in India to 6,500 in 2004; EDS plans to take their number from 600 to 5,000 in the same time frame; and Accenture targets a number of 5,000 from 100.

And why are Convergys, HSBC, Microsoft, Conseco, Toshiba, Fujitsu, Matsushita Electric, and GE aggressively expanding in India and China? GE aims to have 20,000 employees in India by 2003, Conseco now has 1,700 employees, HSBC at 1,100 plans to go up to 2,400, and Convergys at 800 targets a number 1,900. Matsushita Electric has employed about 1,500 Chinese engineers in 2002. Microsoft has software development centers in China. Why do Dell and American Airlines each have 400 employees in Ireland? Why does Hertz have 800? These are figures quoted by a Mckinsey report published jointly with the National Association of Software and Services Companies in India.

All of these companies are looking to reduce costs, gain access to superior talent, improve processes, and focus on their core business activity. And they're all looking offshore. Some companies are offshoring functions from software testing to research and development (R&D). Business processes being offshored range from outbound marketing call centers and stock research to R&D of complex medical equipment.

Over the next five years, India is expected to execute $80 billion worth of business processes, covering about 70 percent of the software and business process offshoring market. China, Ireland, Singapore, Mexico, and the Philippines will capture the rest.

Taking advantage of lower labor costs in these countries is the most compelling factor that drives offshoring. This alone can reduce 60 percent off the cost, and the benefit is sustainable for at least the next 20 years.

Another strong reason to offshore is the need to focus on core business. Companies outsource non-core functions like software development and maintenance, call center operations, trade finance, credit decisions, and human resource processes, to name a few. By exporting these contextual functions, companies can free up valuable resources to concentrate on their core functions.

Retailers like Wal-Mart and JCPenney, whose core function is running efficient retail supply chains, send their transaction processing and call center functions offshore, where they can be cost-effectively managed by an offshore business process service provider. Citibank diverts capital in the US for check-clearing processes, which is now being done offshore. Due to their high degree of specialization, offshore vendors develop process expertise. This leads to continuous improvements in their clients' processes, enabling them to quickly meet changing customer demands.

Offshore outsourcing has given companies access to a highly skilled talent pool, which will not run dry in the foreseeable future. GE has college graduates working at their call centers in India: It would be extremely difficult to source talent of a similar caliber cost-effectively in North America. India graduates numerous software engineers every year: Such a deep pool of talent is difficult to find in North America and Europe.

Offshoring as business strategy is here to stay. Once a company realizes that it is nothing but a conglomeration of business processes, which support its core function, it easily accepts offshoring. For Coca-Cola Company, it is the delivery of the brand's promise. So Coke makes the secret formula and ensures quality standards at the bottlers' plants.

Generally, any company will look to offshoring to:

- cut costs of non-core processes
- focus on core business
- gain access to a high-caliber and cost-effective talent pool
- gain greater internal flexibility

- improve service quality
- make continuous process improvements
- get the benefit of cutting-edge technology

The first wave of outsourcing manufacturing to China and Mexico created new efficiencies; offshoring services will bring the next round of efficiency. Fortune 500 companies are increasingly adopting it for several of their processes. Many smaller companies, too, are finding value in it.

Over the next few years, the corporations discussed in this book will emerge as vibrant entities that create new market realities. The non-believers in offshoring will struggle with flab, as nimble organizations and their outsourcing vendors constantly better efficiencies.

This book is divided into several parts. The first discusses how offshoring software and business process functions has delivered tremendous value to corporations with a global outlook and how a business strategy that excludes offshoring can be detrimental. The second part is a guide through the world of outsourcing and includes information for making decisions about sending software and/or business process functions offshore. The third part is a discussion of the global effects of offshoring. The final part comprises six case studies about four companies that have offshored software and/or business process functions and two companies that provide services.

Chapter 1
The Offshore Imperative

Why is offshore outsourcing crucial for today's businesses? The basic reason is the high price of running contextual processes onshore and the availability of cost-effective solutions offshore. To keep these processes onshore, companies must hire expensive talent, devote management time to non-core activities, lose flexibility in the marketplace, and get diminishing returns on investments. Going offshore solves these problems, especially since offshore vendors can offer sophisticated, quality services.

Six reasons drive offshoring:

- Cost reduction

- Increased focus on core operations

- Improvements in process quality

- Access to a deep talent pool

- More rapid processes and product development

- Product and process innovation

Cost reduction

In a competitive market, companies find they have to look offshore to reduce costs and stay profitable.

The cost of running IT and business processes in the US is high. Between 1995 and 2000, when the US economy was expanding, the cost of developing and maintaining software infrastructure was very high. Corporations could import talent on work visas at rates that were much lower than those of local labor; however, even these rates were higher than wages paid offshore. In the business processing space, US corporations were already outsourcing the payroll processes, contact center operations, data transformation, and even R&D onshore, so there was no reason not to export these offshore at a lower cost.

In a market slowdown, companies spend more to get or retain clients. The incremental costs of this strategy are high, so reducing costs of contact center operations is necessary. In a market slowdown after the salesforce is laid off and capital expenditure reduced, companies look at shared services like HR, benefits, payroll, and administration to reduce costs. But there's a limit to how much shared services can be cut before inefficiencies kick in. The option is to move processes offshore to low-wage islands.

The flexibility of variable costs

To own and run processes requires incurring fixed costs, even if no output is produced. In an economic slowdown, some fixed resources are used during the production period, even with no production. Fixed costs include depreciation due to obsolescence, interest, rent and repairs, taxes, and insurance.

If a company uses debt to set up a call center, for example, it must continue to pay principal and interest, regardless of its output. If the call center is self-financed, there is the opportunity cost of interest on resources that cannot be used elsewhere. If the call center infrastructure is leased, rent must be paid regardless of activity. There are also regular repair and maintenance expenses for the telecom infrastructure and the building, not to mention premium payments for insurance on the building and equipment against hazards, independent of their use.

In a typical boom and bust economic cycle, companies incur huge fixed costs during the expansion phase, aiming to reap high returns. Most companies realize the benefits of these investments, but burden their books with future fixed expenditure. During the contraction phase, as revenues fall, the proportion of fixed costs to revenue increases, putting pressure on the bottom line. Shedding assets in a shrinking economy is difficult, rendering the company inflexible when nimbleness is needed. Only by converting these fixed costs to variable costs will a company be able to manage both boom and bust cycles.

Once they have converted fixed costs to variable, companies incur an additional burden only if there is production. The level of costs depends on the quantity and price of these inputs: they increase as output increases and decrease as output decreases. By moving to a variable cost structure, a company can change the expenses it incurs on such items as rent or technology infrastructure at any time to bring about changes in output. Thus, expense becomes a function of output level.

By moving processes to an offshore vendor, companies take the investment expense off their financial statements. The offshore vendor makes the investments in technology and other infrastructure for a fee from the customer. And the vendor increases or decreases the size of the operation—be it for a call center operation, R&D center, or software development center—based on the needs of the customer. This cushions companies against overcapacity during bust cycles and the need to invest in boom cycles.

GE set up dedicated global development centers (GDCs) in India and selected five offshore vendors to run them. GE ensured that the GDCs got enough business to keep them profitable; although these centers cater solely to GE, the company has no equity stake in them, and the vendor bears the risk of under-utilization.

Slashing absolute costs

The reduction in absolute costs to free up capital for investment in new initiatives is one of the strongest reasons to send processes offshore. Outsourcing processes within the country can bring down costs, but nowhere near the level of outsourcing offshore. Offshoring taps into the surplus talent in countries like India and China with their low cost of labor. Shifting software development to an offshore center can cut costs by as much as 70 percent on some technology platforms. For low-end business process outsourcing (BPO) projects, offshoring brings down costs by nearly 50 percent. Faced with high costs for running call centers in North America, GE moved the process offshore to get the cost down.

Because they fully own the offshore centers and the cost remains on their balance sheets, corporations like Citibank Bank are unable to move from a fixed to a variable cost structure. Therefore, absolute cost reduction is key. Exporting development to an offshore subsidiary can bring down costs, but bears the risk of excess inventory during busts and difficulty meeting peak demands.

Maximum benefits accrue when the entire function outsourced and all the work is performed offshore. Citibank saves about $75 million a year by outsourcing its trade finance, check processing, customer services, loans, bills, credit cards, and cash management processes. British Airways cut costs by $42 million on its passenger revenue accounting, error handling, and miles-tracking processes.

When Amazon.com wanted to reduce costs of its contact center operations, it outsourced the process to Daksh, a BPO provider in India. Cutting costs by at least 60 percent gave the company a much-needed boost. Amazon.com claims that the move enabled it to leverage India's high-quality and cost-effective customer care professionals.

For GE, cost was an important driver to offshoring. GE gets a cost advantage of nearly 25 percent for low-end services and as high as 60 percent for the processes up the value chain. By 2005, the offshoring initiative will deliver an annualized savings of $1 billion.

Shifting production bases offshore for labor cost alone is not always the best solution. As economies develop, labor costs rise quickly and erode cost benefits. With the loss of proximity to markets, this can make offshore production bases a drag on any company, particularly for capital-intensive manufacturing companies. No wonder Japanese automobile manufacturers like Toyota and Honda have set up plants in North America and Europe.

But manufacturing is poles apart from business processing and software development in cost metrics. In manufacturing, labor costs are 15 to 20 percent of the total. On the other hand, labor accounts for nearly 75 percent of the costs of developing software and running business process operations like accounting and contact centers. Since labor accounts for a major chunk of running business processes, moving to low-wage islands like India, China, and Russia brings tremendous cost advantages.

A software project manager earns about $90,000 a year in the US and just $30,000 in India—certainly a compelling argument for offshore software development. A call center employee earns around $30,000 in the US and $8,000 in India. Accountants earn about $50,000 in the US versus $10,000 to $15,000 in India.

There is another cost benefit of shifting software development offshore. Competition among vendors in the offshore BPO and the software space has put pressure on pricing. Even though quality service providers are few, the number of companies responding to requests for proposals compels top-notch players to reduce prices. However, companies offshoring processes have realized that price is not the only decision-making factor. Long-term financial viability and quality of the vendor are equally important.

In India alone, there are over 3,000 software service providers, of which 25 generate 60 percent of the software sector's revenues. To win business in the international markets, these vendors compete fiercely on rates. And joining in a rate war are software service providers in China, Russia, Ireland, and Israel.

Another cost advantage in offshore outsourcing is currency appreciation. The dollar has been appreciating against the rupee, ruble, and yuan. This enables customers to demand rate reductions. GECIS, the outsourcing arm of GE, credits the process owner with the profits made every year. As costs decrease, the profit credit increases. The constant reduction in rates frees up money to be spent on new technology, which keeps companies ahead in the marketplace.

India meets a major chunk of IT outsourcing requirements and has emerged as a leader in the BPO space. The Indian rupee (INR) has been depreciating for some time and is expected to continue its downward trend. India depends on exports for its economic well-being, so worked to prevent any appreciation of the INR. The INR that stood at 42.5 to the US dollar in December 1998 fell to around 45 in November 2003. With the US economy picking up, the dollar will begin appreciating again.

IDG, the technology research company, predicts that in 2005, $17.5 billion of IT work will be outsourced offshore out of a total outsourcing of $100 billion to take advantage of the cost differential. And what can be achieved in the $17.5 billion will be much greater than today, given the falling rates and depreciating offshore currencies.

Increased focus on core operations

The second strongest reason for outsourcing offshore is to increase focus on core competencies. All outsourcing decisions must consider: What is the company's core expertise? Where is management time and scarce capital best used? What is the opportunity cost of adding another area of responsibility or of being distracted from the core capability?

Outsourcing allows organizations to focus on their core competencies. According to management guru C.K. Prahalad, core competencies are the collective learning in the organization that entails co-ordination of production skills and integrates multiple streams of technology. Core competencies are skill and knowledge sets, not products or functions. They must be flexible, long-term platforms for success. Limited to about three to five, they exist as unique sources of leverage in the value chain. They are in areas where the company can dominate the competition and are embedded in the organization's systems.

Leveraging core competencies through strategic alliances enhances an organization's competitive edge in the marketplace. To bring a wider array of books and music to its customers, Amazon.com teamed up with Borders. Prahalad advocates that organizations cultivate a core competency mind-set: Competency-savvy managers work well across organizational boundaries, willingly share resources, and think long term. To encourage this mind-set, the organization has to stop thinking of business units as sacrosanct. That only imprisons resources in units and motivates managers to hide talent as the company pursues hot opportunities. He argues that the companies identify projects and people who embody the firm's core competencies as it sends a message that core competencies are corporate—not unit—resources and those who embody them can be re-allocated. Benefiting from core focus also entails identifying next-generation competencies and allocating capital and staff from units.

Focusing on core competencies involves substantial commitment from the organization. First, the organization has to identify and communicate them throughout the company. Management must then fine-tune the systems of the company to enable it to support the area of competency. The core competency then goes on to serve the markets in which the company operates.

Once it has identified the core competencies, the company has to build on them. This entails investing in technologies, R&D, and market research to strengthen the organization's competency, to build global brands and a portfolio of products to dominate a market segment. It requires access to new distribution channels and strengthening customer relationships.

When the commitment required of management time and capital resources to focus on core competencies is identified, it is clear that contextual processes must be shed, and so the company looks at ways to run them without eating into corporate resources. This is where outsourcing comes in. It was the need to focus on core that drove outsourcing in the early 1990s. Outsourcing offshore, on the other hand, was driven by the need to focus on core cost-effectiveness.

A successful outsourcing relationship enables companies to focus their people and resources, which are sometimes scarce, on the areas that add the most value to the organization. It also gives these companies access to the top talent in an outsourced discipline, talent that the client company doesn't have to recruit, train, pay benefits for, or struggle to retain, thereby freeing up management time.

Companies cannot afford to allocate time to non-core activities. When competition outsources contextual functions offshore and establishes a stronger position in its core markets, offshoring is hard to ignore. For example, the key activities for biotechnology companies are the discovery, development, and marketing of products. If they were to carry out all the manufacturing for these in-house, their whole operation would become skewed towards this high-asset/overhead/resource activity and away from those competencies that they actually exist to pursue. Other key factors for the pharmaceuticals industry are the ever-increasing regulatory burden on manufacturers and the sheer scale of operation required, when only one in 5,000 compounds that are researched actually make it to market. Hence, it does not make sense for a biotechnology company to own high overheads.

When ABN AMRO looked at its core competencies, it saw that several contextual processes like bills and accounts reconciliation were far removed from the core, so the bank offshored them. For retailers, the core area should be superlative supply-chain management to keep inventory at the minimum but ensure that customers get the goods they need. It makes no sense for Amazon.com to run a call center operation, which is essentially a contextual function, in the US. Amazon.com has outsourced its contact center operations to India, so it can invest management time and money in connecting to a greater number of suppliers.

As companies realize the need to concentrate on core, they also realize that contextual functions are not worth significant investments of capital or management time. However, these processes are critical to the running of core functions and need to be run cost-effectively and efficiently. To deal with the Y2K problem, Northwestern Mutual had to focus on new initiatives. But the IT talent crunch meant that the resources to build new IT systems were not available; therefore, it brought in offshore vendors and was able to build IT systems to enter new avenues of business.

Outsourcing takes the focus on core to a new level. What is contextual to an organization is core to its outsourcing vendor. Therefore, outsourcing results in great service improvements as non-core, but essential, work is handed to best-in-class outside providers. The strategic benefits include greater value, higher service levels, lower costs, innovation, and business partnerships that encourage new thinking and introduce new ideas. Outsourcing maintains and even strengthens the competitive advantages of both the vendor and the outsourcer. Northwestern Mutual was able to enter new related market segments as it outsourced IT development to an offshore vendor. Firms have benefited from outsourcing payroll systems, distribution and logistics, IT, and call centers.

The relationship with an external service provider has greater benefits than the association with an internal unit providing the same service. The external service provider is motivated to expand the relationship by improving processes and exploring fresh avenues to add more value. At GE, the managers of various units find that with no capital investment, GECIS, GE's in-house vendor in India, provides the best-in-class service by recommending changes and executing quality improvements internal units did not think of.

Improvements in process quality

Exporting non-core functions to a vendor undoubtedly improves process quality because the vendor focuses on its area of competency—the very processes it is running. Offshore vendors make constant improvements in processes by using quality tools and submitting to frequent mandatory audits by independent bodies.

It is highly unlikely that an organization would apply these tools rigorously to contextual processes. A mortgage company, for example, would rather focus its attention on improving the quality of its selling rather than its back-office reconciliation function, which may end up a broken process. However, exporting the process ensures that it is fixed, as running the process efficiently is the core competency of the vendor.

Six Sigma rigor

The Six Sigma measure of quality is a disciplined, data-driven approach to eliminate defects in a product or process. A successful Six Sigma service will have six standard deviations between the mean and the nearest specification limit. This means that no production process or service will have more than 3.4 defect parts per million (PPM) opportunities, or defects per million opportunities (DPMO), to be produced. Anything outside a customer's specification is a Six Sigma defect. (In comparison, a level of Five Sigma means 233 DPMO; One Sigma is 690,000.)

When an existing process does not meet customer specification or is not performing adequately, Six Sigma practitioners fix the problem by DMAIC:

- Define the project goals and the internal and external customer deliverables.
- Measure the process to determine current performance.
- Analyze and determine the root causes of the defects.
- Improve the process by eliminating defects.
- Control future process performance.

If the vendor plans to develop a new product or process, or if an existing product or process has been optimized and still doesn't meet the level of customer specification or Six Sigma level, the quality team will use DMADV:

- Define the project goals and customer (internal and external) deliverables.
- Measure and determine customer needs and specifications.
- Analyze the process options to meet the customer needs.
- Design in detail the process to meet the customer needs.
- Verify the design performance and ability to meet customer needs.

Implementing Six Sigma results in substantial cost savings. Since an organization does not invest time to improve contextual processes, these savings are not realized in non-core functions until they are exported offshore and the vendor takes the process to a higher sigma level.

On a global basis, Motorola saved about $16 billion between 1986 and 2001, Allied Signal $500 million in 1998, GE $4.4 billion between 1996 and 1999, and Honeywell $1.8 billion between 1998 and 2000. These savings represent from 1.2 to 4.5 percent of revenue for these companies

CMM SEI process maturity

Most software companies in India use the capability maturity model (CMM) of Carnegie Mellon's Software Engineering Institute (SEI), an American-based measure of quality. CMM helps software organizations measure and improve the maturity of their software processes. It is organized into five maturity levels, and several Indian software companies are at the highest level 5, ensuring that their software code is much better than the code created by programmers in North America or Europe.

The five levels of quality described by the SEI are:

1. Initial: The software process is characterized as ad hoc and even chaotic. Few processes are defined, and success depends on individual effort.

2. Repeatable: Basic project-management processes are established to track cost, schedule, and function. Process discipline is in place to repeat earlier successes on projects with similar applications.

3. Defined: The software process for both management and engineering activities is documented, standardized, and integrated into a standard software process for the organization. All projects use an approved, tailored version of the organization's standard process for developing and maintaining software.

4. Managed: Detailed measures of the software process and product quality are collected. Software process and products are quantitatively understood and controlled.

5. Optimizing: Continuous process improvement is enabled by quantitative feedback from the process and from piloting innovative ideas and technologies.

Predictability, effectiveness, and control of an organization's software processes improve as the organization moves up these five levels.

Except for level 1, each maturity level is decomposed into several key process areas that indicate the areas an organization should focus on to improve its software process. At level 2, these focus on the software project's concerns related to establishing basic project-management controls: requirements management, software project planning, software project tracking and oversight, software subcontract management, software quality assurance, and software configuration management.

The key process areas at level 3 address both project and organizational issues: organization process focus, organization process definition, training program, integrated software management, software product engineering, inter-group co-ordination, and peer reviews. At level 4, they focus on establishing a quantitative understanding of both software process and software products: quantitative process management and software quality management.

The key process areas at level 5 cover the issues that both the organization and the projects must address to implement continual, measurable software process improvement: defect prevention, technology change management, and process change management.

ISO certifications

The ISO 9001:2000 standard is an internationally recognized quality management system developed by the International Organization of Standardization (ISO). The ISO process emphasizes the incorporation of quality standards into systems, procedures, documentation, and total employee involvement. To be ISO-certified, an organization has to implement a quality management system covering the design, development, quality assurance, testing, and release procedures of software products and services. With 140 countries working in partnership, ISO facilitates the international exchange of goods and services by promoting the development of standards that remove technical barriers for similar products.

ISO 9001 streamlines productivity and reduces waste, which decreases production costs and increases profitability. It improves product quality and reliability to increase customer satisfaction. Vendors use it as a tool to increase productivity, improve communications, promote teamwork, improve performance, and achieve quality goals. ISO 9001:2000 is a series of quality assurance standards (published in 1987 and modified in 1994 and 2000) to provide a common worldwide set of quality system guidelines and requirements. More than 200 countries, including the US, have adopted ISO 9001 as the national quality standard. ISO 9001 is the first consistent set of international standards available to evaluate a company's ability to provide a quality product.

To implement ISO standards, an organization must have:

- a quality council that meets to determine and discuss quality levels and means for improvement
- a formal organizational structure with a quality policy manual, standard operating procedures, and work instructions for all critical functions of the process
- a specification book containing specific formulas for products
- formal training and communication meetings on a continuing basis
- a formal procedure for order review to ensure customer satisfaction
- complete record keeping to guarantee reproducibility of a product or service
- formal corrective/preventive action programs
- continuous finished product testing
- a formal customer complaint procedure
- a formal internal audit procedure to verify compliance with the program

Most software vendors in India have both CMM SEI and ISO certifications.

Access to a deep talent pool

Cost is a function of supply and demand. Companies in countries like the US face a shortage of software professionals, so they must pay them a premium, face losses as they move to better-paying jobs, and constantly import more. On the other hand, companies in countries like India and China have access to huge pools of software professionals. Shifting development to areas offshore with a surplus of talent takes away the uncertainty in getting resources at critical times.

What is true of software engineers is also true of call center representatives, accountants, HR professionals, and scientists. The supply of these professionals is much higher in India than anywhere else in the world. For high-end processes like R&D, talent pool access is of greater importance than cost reduction. This is one of the reasons GE and Microsoft set up R&D centers in India.

The shortage of talent in developed countries and the cost-effective and abundant supply in countries like Russia, India, and China makes offshoring the solution. It is not just the quantity but the quality of talent that prompts offshore outsourcing. Graduates in India run call centers, unlike in the US. Says Meera Sanyal of ACES: "The voluntary retirement schemes launched by nationalized banks in India has led to a lot of surplus banking talent. These people have over 20 years of banking experience, and by establishing shop in India, ABN AMRO has been able to access this top-quality talent." To read more about the bank's experience, see "The ABN AMRO Story".

According to IDG, the gap between the number of IT workers needed in the US and the number actually employed was about 330,000 in 2002, up from 72,003 in 1995. That scarcity is driving an increasing number of companies to use some offshore IT services. IDG estimates that over $17.5 billion of IT work will be outsourced offshore by 2005 out of the total IT outsourcing of $100 billion. The US will continue to spend the most on IT outsourcing services, accounting for 44 percent in 2005. Western Europe is increasing spending by 10.3 percent a year, from $16 billion in 2000 to more than $26 billion in 2005. Pacific Rim IT outsourcing spending will grow 20 percent from 2000 to 2005.

As the need for talent increases, so will cost. The US Department of Commerce analyzed Bureau of Labor Statistics (BLS) growth projections for the three core occupational classifications of IT workers—computer scientists and engineers, systems analysts, and computer programmers—to assess future US demand. BLS projections indicated that between 1996 and 2006, the US will require more than 1.3 million new IT workers in these three occupations—an average of about 137,800 per year—to fill newly created jobs (1,134,000) and to replace workers who are leaving these fields (244,000) as a result of retirement, change of professions, or other reasons.

The largest growth in jobs will be for systems analysts, projected to increase 103 percent from 506,000 in 1996 to 1,025,000 in 2006. The projected increase for all other professions is 14 percent. The number of computer engineers and scientists is expected to grow by 114 percent, from 427,000 to 912,000, over the same period, while the number of computer programmer positions is expected to grow at a slower 23 percent, from 567,000 in 1996 to 697,000 in 2006. However, while only 129,000 new computer programmer jobs are created during this period, 177,000 new programmers will be required to replace those exiting the occupation.

What does this mean? First, the shortage will mean higher wages. Second, inexperienced programmers entering the industry can lead to poor quality.

Computer and data processing are growing in their IT worker intensity. It is projected that by 2006, 41.3 percent of this industry's employees will be computer programmers, systems analysts, and computer scientists and engineers. An increase in the wages of software engineers will badly skew the wage bill of IT-intensive companies as they form a large chunk of the workforce. And the shortage of IT workers will put the core functions of these companies at risk.

The problem goes beyond IT-intensive industries to verticals that employ a large number of IT workers. The US government is projected to be less IT intensive in 2006 than many other industries, but the sheer size of its IT workforce (96,704) would make a tight IT labor market a serious problem. Other IT-intensive industries include insurance, banking, financial services, and telecommunications.

Many people who work in skilled IT jobs have educational backgrounds other than computer science and engineering. According to 1993 data from the National Science Foundation, about one-third of people working in computer programming hold degrees in computer science, and about one-quarter of those in computer and information sciences hold computer and information science degrees. Other workers in these fields hold degrees in such areas as business, social sciences, mathematics, engineering, psychology, economics, and education. This poses a quality risk, as the IT workers with a computer science background can do better work than a programmer with a psychology degree. The vast supply of computer science graduates eliminates this problem in countries like India.

The problem is slightly different in the BPO space, where the US has adequate talent to supply labor. Moving business processes offshore, however, gains access to a wider talent pool. India has a population of more than one billion, of whom 300 million speak English. More than six million people are enrolled in the 200 universities, 5,000 colleges, and 100,000 secondary schools. The BPO space needs knowledge workers with a minimum education level of a Bachelor of Commerce or Arts or Science. India churns out graduates at a rate much higher than the US or Europe. The result is that companies going offshore get more-qualified workers.

India, the leader in offshore IT outsourcing, provides a solution for the global labor shortage with its vast resource of skilled software human power. The number of technology schools has led to a strong growth in the number of India's IT professionals over the last decade. NASSCOM, the association of Indian software companies, says that from a base of 6,800 knowledge workers in 1985–1986, the number increased to 522,000 software and services professionals by the end of 2001–2002. It estimates that almost 170,000 are working in the IT software and services export industry; nearly 106,000 in the IT-enabled services, and over 220,000 in user organizations. For more information on India's talent pool, see chapter 7.

Government and industry in India are taking steps to meet these requirements and prevent the projected shortage of knowledge workers. China, too, is taking steps to create a large talent pool to meet the demand for knowledge workers, as it starts to emerge as a large provider of offshore outsourcing services.

More rapid processes and product development

Exporting processes offshore increases the speed of product and service delivery for two reasons: access to a deep talent pool and time zone differences. Access to a ready pool of resources enables a quick ramp-up of activity that leads to faster delivery. For instance, in a software project, it is much easier to get resources in India than in North America, and the same is true of call centers or data entry operations.

The time zone difference enables faster development cycles and quicker time-to-market of software and R&D projects. When the workday is over at an offshore development center, the code can be handed over to programmers working in a different time zone. This allows companies to run 16 to 24 hours of programming a day without paying overtime. GE conducts R&D on a project out of centers in India, China, and the US. The engineers work on different aspects of a product in different time zones, which leads to simultaneous product development.

Distributed development teams have established periodic project reviews, which identify project gaps between different development centers. They provide project status to the project managers and identify actions needed to move forward. These reviews are key for the successful 24/7 operations in distributed development.

Product and process innovation

Rapid technological change results in increased expenses to upgrade systems, time to install, and complexity to master. For a company whose IT department is a non-core function, maintaining a best-in-class status under these conditions is next to impossible, especially for small and medium enterprises where cost is a critical factor. These factors have led IT outsourcing to experience extremely rapid growth over recent years.

The experiences of companies that have sent processes offshore show that Indian counterparts assist in actual product development. Microsoft India played a key role in developing several products for its parent's portfolio, including Visual J#.Net, three versions of the Windows Services for UNIX (SFU) product, and Outlook 2002 Connector. Indian offshore centers of such other companies as Compaq-HP, Oracle, and GE have contributed to the creation of new innovative products in the market.

Citibank's Latin American operations had country-focused IT with redundant systems and functions: Going offshore changed that as the vendor moved Citibank to a robust client server technology. For more information on the bank's experience, see "The Citibank Story".

Conclusion

Today, there is no argument against moving processes offshore to gain cost, quality, and speed benefits. The offshore model meets the requirements of the demand side: cost, quality, speed, and access to a wide talent pool. On the supply side, providers have a mature delivery model that clinches the offshore outsourcing argument.

The fact that going offshore can reduce costs by at least 35 percent is hard to ignore. So is moving from a fixed to a variable cost structure and the flexibility it provides. These two cost factors release substantial capital, which a company can use in its core business. Besides cost benefits in moving contextual processes offshore, companies are able to focus on their core activities. In today's competitive marketplace, no company can afford to divert resources to non-core processes. Also moving non-core processes offshore gives these functions the attention a core process should get because the non-core processes are actually core for the offshore vendor.

As the contextual processes are core to the vendor, they get the management time and attention that leads to quality improvements. Also as most vendors measure quality standards with models like Six Sigma and CMM SEI, processes sent offshore see dramatic improvements in quality. Improvements in contextual processes eventually benefit the core process, and as processes improve, the cost of running them falls.

Access to a deep and wide talent pool overseas provides cost savings, focus on core, quality improvements, speed and scale, and innovation. To access this pool, US and European companies must export processes, as bringing this talent pool on-site is too difficult due to immigration rules. Once the project moves offshore, it can ramp up operations quickly due to access to local talent.

Chapter 2
The Total Cost of Offshoring

Offshore outsourcing touches organizations, people, and nations, bringing with it great benefits but also upheaval and pain. It cuts costs by decoupling processes, provides jobs overseas by laying off people on-site, spurs angry street protests, and provokes legislation to prevent the export of processes. Offshoring is inevitable in today's global business environment, which encourages free flow of capital, goods, and services but prevents cross-border movement of talent.

The previous chapter on "The Offshore Imperative" outlined the benefits of outsourcing offshore, but there are costs.

Financial costs—tangible and intangible

Offshoring vendors and consultants want companies' business. They will say that offshore outsourcing can reduce costs by 80 percent, a saving that is achieved only rarely and simply represents the difference in labor costs. But there is more to offshoring than labor arbitrage. Companies should calculate the total cost of offshoring, including vendor selection expenses, management time devoted to vendor management, loss of goodwill, and the risk of handing over critical processes to an offshore vendor. However, the final sum is always better after offshoring.

Capturing recurring costs

Although management needs to spend less time on non-core tasks with offshore outsourcing, it must still devote time to control and supervise the functions. Most companies do not book these recurring costs, as they are not immediately tangible. It is also difficult to estimate them, as management time required not only depends on the complexity of problems but also is discontinuous. However, it is important to capture these costs to give an accurate picture of the benefits of offshore outsourcing. Hence the costs incurred in managing the process should be apportioned.

The time a company devotes to governance and supervision also must be added into the total cost of offshoring. Vendors claim high-quality work and point out their CMM level 5, Six Sigma, and ISO certifications, but proper governance is important in all outsourcing engagements to ensure that buyers receive the quality implied in the certifications. And as projects move overseas, there must be strong supervision for data security and intellectual property protection. The level of supervision on-site can be on a much lower scale, as all processes are in one physical location. But with offshore governance, costs are higher.

The other recurring cost is payments made to the vendor for the services delivered. This is always factored into the total cost of outsourcing as it is built into the contract and is tangible, unlike the management time spent on the offshoring initiative. This recurring cost is much lower than the cost of keeping the process on-site and is a variable cost for the customer, as the vendor bears all the fixed costs.

One-time costs

The highest one-time costs incurred in an offshoring project are for vendor appraisal and selection, and process transition. Vendor appraisal and selection tasks include: requesting information, requesting proposals, evaluating proposals and vendors, selecting the vendor, and preparing the contract. Other one-time costs are associated with determining which processes to send offshore and then exporting them.

Vendor selection requires a lot of expensive senior management time. Some companies also pay consultants to help select vendors by evaluating, negotiating, and implementing outsourcing transactions. Using the services of a consultant is generally a one-time cost, unless the company decides to use the consultant throughout the life of the offshoring contract.

Management has to allocate the time to decide which processes recommended by the vendor or its own staff should be outsourced. This entails going through the recommendations in detail and weighing the pros and cons. After selecting the processes for offshoring, the customer must pay for training the vendor's employees in them, and the longer it takes to train, the higher the cost. If the training takes place on the client's site, it can wipe out almost 30 to 50 percent of the first year's cost savings, depending on the complexity of the process. Then, in decoupling functions and moving them overseas, processes can be broken. Until processes are running smoothly overseas, the customer has to back them up on-site. Once the process stabilizes offshore, there is the final cost of winding down the on-site overheads.

Some of these one-time costs recur if new processes are offshored—with discovery, transition, and knowledge transfer.

Calculating transactional costs

To arrive at the total cost of outsourcing, a company must tabulate expenses on a transactional basis. This is unlike effort-based costing, in which the company simply calculates the number of hours the line workers and their managers spend on a process, works out the cost based on the wages on-site and offshore, determines the difference between the wages, and arrives at the cost savings.

Transactional costing captures quantified cost and time data, measures process and activity performance, and determines the cost of business process outputs. It captures organizational costs for the factors of production and administrative expenses, and applies them to the defined activity structure. In an offshoring initiative, the transactional costs should include IT infrastructure costs, communication costs, costs on property overseas, wages, and the management time.

Adding these costs, the savings on offshore is not so dramatic. For instance, in a call center operation, the savings on labor alone are as high as 80 percent. However, once all the transaction costs are added, the saving comes down to about 35 percent. Offshore outsourcing provides benefits in terms of cost, even after taking the transactional expenses into account. But before entering the offshore space, companies should be aware of the total cost of outsourcing.

Non-financial costs—unpredictable and real

People seek the best value for their money by purchasing the least expensive and best-quality goods and services. Similarly, corporations look for the most cost-effective way to deliver high-quality goods and services to meet that demand. When regulation prevents cost-effective local access to talent and quality, corporations look overseas. This dramatic shift causes medium-term pain to local labor but is a catalyst to robust global trade. In the meantime, there are additional non-financial costs that are hard to predict and may or may not crystallize.

Risk of goodwill loss

Outsourcing leads to a loss of goodwill among employees due to lay-offs, when the media give wide and negative publicity to outsourcing deals by quoting ex-employees. This not only damages the company's own image but also that of the outsourcing vendors. The backlash against outsourcing is growing, as a wide range of high-tech and service-sector jobs move out of the US. People who have lost jobs to offshore employees take to the streets, and the media cover these protests.

According to media reports, in June 2003, at an offshore outsourcing conference at the Waldorf-Astoria in New York, 125 executives heard consultants describe how companies could lower costs by shifting such tasks as computer programming, accounting, and procurement to India, the Philippines, China, Malaysia, and elsewhere in the developing world. Outside the hotel, high-tech workers with advanced degrees but no jobs marched in protest, carried signs with slogans like "Outsourcing Is Stealing Billion$ From America." Several passersby were giving them the thumbs up. The media quoted protesters saying that people can't find jobs because foreign workers are taking them all. They also quoted reports from Forrester Research and other research firms, which estimate that, by 2015, 3.36 million jobs, worth about $136 billion annually in wages, will have moved offshore, as US employers look for ways to reduce salary costs and office rents.

No company wants to be caught in the middle of a national outcry over its offshore outsourcing. First, its disgruntled ex-employees will talk to the media and erode its goodwill. And it will risk having talent in the core areas taking flight in anticipation of job loss. Therefore, any company looking at offshoring must use public relations to send a positive message to employees and the media—even though offshore outsourcing causes initial job losses, it strengthens the US economy by lowering costs and giving companies the flexibility to hire and fire the offshore vendor's employees as business conditions change. To prevent the backlash, it must convey all the benefits of offshore outsourcing: the ability to focus on core, boosting profits; the cost-effective availability of talent; job creation in developing countries, which will now be able to buy goods and services from the US, creating job opportunities for US labor in future.

Managing the media and loss of employee goodwill takes management time and money, possibly requiring the use of a professional PR firm, one cost that companies never take into account when moving processes offshore. It is easy to measure this cost in monetary terms and add it to the total cost of offshoring; however, it is impossible to forecast the actual money that the company will have to spend, as that will depend on the extent of the backlash against it. And the backlash depends on several factors. During the initial phases of outsourcing from 1995 to 2000, the economy was booming and the scale of offshore outsourcing was small; therefore, US labor did not feel the pain of job loss. That is no longer the case, as the economy continues to trudge along and companies desperately want to cut costs by offshoring.

Legislative blockades

Protesters are lobbying Congress to restrict offshoring, possibly by imposing surcharges on outsourced work to discourage the use of foreign labor and tightening limits on foreign-worker visas. Their pitch is that every job lost is a lost taxpayer. The media quotes protesters saying that the anti-offshoring movement is picking up steam nationwide. Lobbying to prevent changes in the laws that create hurdles in offshore outsourcing will have costs that are much higher than dealing with the media and employees.

Outsourcing has started drawing attention on Capitol Hill, where the House Small Business Committee is examining the practice. The committee's chairman, Rep Donal ManZullo, stated: "The US economy is growing and creating jobs; it's just not Americans filling those jobs. They have been moved overseas, where foreigners will work for a lot less."

With the growing publicity of job losses, politicians are moving in to protect American labor. The New Jersey bill to prevent offshore outsourcing is one attempt to stop state government jobs from going offshore. In March 2002, New Jersey state senator Shirley Turner introduced a bill to provide that only citizens or legal residents of the US may be employed in performing certain state contracts. "Recent published reports have indicated that telephone inquiries by welfare and food stamp clients under New Jersey's Families First Program were being handled by operators in Bombay, India after the contractor moved its operations outside of the United States as a cost-cutting measure. The bill is intended to ensure that State funds are used to employ people residing in the United States and to prevent the loss of jobs to foreign countries," the bill stated.

In December 2002, the state senate passed the bill, which still needs to be approved by the assembly and signed into law by the governor. Although the Turner bill is yet to be law, concerns and pressures faced by the state from unemployed workers and the media have already affected one BPO deal. New Jersey awarded an Arizona-based outsourcing company eFunds Corp. a seven-year, $326,000-monthly contract to process electronic benefits transfer and food stamp cards for about 200,000 New Jersey residents. After getting the contract, eFunds moved the related work from a facility in Green Bay, Wisconsin, to India. However, due to controversy, the State of New Jersey asked eFunds to staff a NJ call center with US citizens, even though they had to renegotiate the contract. The increase in cost is about 20 percent over the original contracted amount, or $886,000 a year.

State officials explained to the media: "The concern was larger than the economics: we operate a welfare system that requires people to work and at the same time we can't tell them that we're taking entry level jobs out of this economy."

Champions of offshore outsourcing cite cost benefits of going offshore. They point out that a bill banning offshoring can have several implications. For one, the New Jersey bill increases costs to the taxpayer because it can prevent that state from awarding contracts to the lowest global bidder.

New Jersey state assemblyman Upendra Chivukula, a Democrat, quoted in an e-mail exchange with IDG News Service, said: "Given the increasingly interconnected economies around the world, the bill could have a variety of unintended consequences.... Most of the largest financial companies, such as Merrill Lynch and Goldman Sachs, have overseas operations and perform financial data modeling overseas. If New Jersey wants to do bond financing, it needs to use one of those companies. But it can't as per the requirements of this bill."

Chivukula feels that rather than restricting the use of foreign labor, policy makers should find a way to reInvest the savings achieved through lower-cost global labor to create higher paying jobs in the US. But in the short run, politicians reacting to the job loss in their voter base, try to pass laws preventing offshore outsourcing. For now the New Jersey bill has been put on the back burner.

Chapter 3
The Short-Sighted Strategy of Not Offshoring

As companies offshore processes and gain the benefits or hurt from upheaval, companies not offshoring are directly affected by the changes in the marketplace for goods, services, and talent. In the final analysis, sending processes offshore is better in the long run, as the short-term benefits erode quickly.

Short-term benefits of not offshoring

The benefits of not offshoring are all short term. And they are quickly neutralized once competition moves processes offshore and provides the market with better-quality products and services at a lower cost. Keeping processes onshore to retain employee goodwill, avoid the pain of change management, and save money otherwise spent on the vendor selection process is a recipe for disaster.

Keeping processes on-site means that employees will not lose their jobs and the company will not face negative publicity. Management will not have to devote time and money to handle a public relations campaign. However, once competition steps in, this strategy will backfire. First, competition will provide goods and services at better price and quality levels, which will eat into the market share of companies that have not offshored. The resulting shrinking revenue base will result in higher marginal costs of running contextual functions. Eventually, jobs in non-core functions that were saved by not going offshore will be lost. But the problem now runs much deeper. Since the company is losing market share, its very existence may be threatened, and many other people will lose jobs.

When processes are exported overseas, companies have to go through the laborious processes of decoupling functions, sending them overseas, and ensuring optimum knowledge transfer. Companies not offshoring will enjoy the pleasure of status quo. This again is short lived. Once competition forces the company to move processes offshore, the pain of exporting will be greater, as it tries to catch up to avoid losing market share. The short time to catch up may result in broken processes. Also the effort involved to move the process will be much higher than in the case of the first mover.

Another short-term benefit of not offshoring is saving time and money that would be spent on appraising and selecting an offshore vendor. Management spends substantial effort in the offshoring process—in vendor appraisal and selection and in knowledge transfer. Some companies spend the money to hire a consulting firm to help the offshoring process. However, once competition begins to gain the benefit of offshoring, others have to follow quickly to catch up. This eventually proves to be more expensive and fraught with risks than making the first move.

Costs of not offshoring

The cost of not outsourcing offshore is prohibitive, entailing recruiting and paying high salaries for workers on-site, increasing costs for supervision, loss of goodwill and market share to competition providing better service by going offshore. The benefits of not outsourcing are short term: The company will not lose the goodwill of its employees and vendors on-site nor face the short-term pain of change when processes are exported offshore, and it saves the time and money that it would have spent on appraising and selecting an offshore vendor.

The cost of not offshoring is being left behind. As competition cuts cost, improves quality and speed to market, has access to a deep and wide talent pool, and concentrates resources on core competencies, companies staying on-site will lose market share. A company not outsourcing will avoid the short-term pain that offshoring brings, but, in the long run, it will lose the competitive edge that sustains its place in the market.

High financial cost

Retaining processes on-site prevents companies from reducing their operational costs, as they cannot take advantage of the low labor costs overseas. These companies are also unable to move from a fixed to a variable cost structure, making them inflexible—running the risk of under-using capital resources during a slowdown and unable to ramp up capital equipment quickly enough during boom times to meet increasing demand. Keeping investment costs on the company's books also reduces its flexibility in the marketplace.

The absolute costs of keeping the process on-site are prohibitive. This high cost will ultimately trickle down to the final customer, who may be unwilling to pay a high price, given that competition that has outsourced processes offers the same goods and services at a lower price.

Loss of focus on core

With high overheads and numerous non-core processes retained in-house by a company not offshoring, management has neither the time nor money to focus on its core activity, thereby risking a loss of its competitive edge. The company is further weakened by competition that has offshored processes and poured cash and other resources into its core business, thus gaining an edge in the marketplace with new products and services.

Not only does keeping contextual functions on-site prevent companies from focusing on core, but also non-core functions do not get any attention at all. This leads to broken processes that eventually will affect the core processes.

Limited access to talent

Not going offshore means that a company will face a shortage of talent and, consequently, incur a high cost for recruiting people. According to the US Department of Commerce, the US will be short by 1.3 million IT professionals—computer scientists and engineers, systems analysts, and computer programmers—by 2006.

The talent shortage continues even after the technology slump. It also affects other business processes like R&D, accounting, and call centers. With little availability of talent, no innovation-based company can be expected to survive in the marketplace: Not globalizing R&D processes will take away their competitive edge.

The accounting profession is also facing a shortage in the US. Deloitte Touche Tohmatsu chief James Copeland recently noted that attracting sufficient numbers of talented people to the accounting profession in the years ahead was an area of concern. Citing demographic and population trends (specifically the baby boom generation that is beginning to retire) and the potential impact of new accounting legislation, he indicated that recruiting and retaining the highly specialized competencies and expertise required to audit global companies may be very difficult. "America's capital markets demand a steady supply of top-notch

35

talent. The accounting profession will be challenged in the years ahead to attract and retain the caliber of professionals required to fulfill the responsibilities with which it is entrusted." Unless companies move non-core accounting processes offshore, they will be hit by the talent shortage in this space.

In the call center space, companies suffer from very high attrition. Call center operations often touch the end customers, and attrition means that employees do not gain the knowledge to serve industry-specific customers effectively. This can eventually lead to a loss of the customer, who expects a certain level of service and may be getting it from an offshore call center.

No quality focus

By not offshoring functions in non-core areas, companies lose out on quality. Since the offshore processes are core for the vendor, they get the required quality focus there. A company retaining an insurance claims process on-site with poor quality is bound to lose business to a company that has a superior and cost-effective quality process delivered by an offshore vendor.

Loss of speed

Offshore outsourcing has increased the speed to market to several companies, a result of work on the project never stopping. As competition gets products into the market earlier, companies not offshoring will face loss in market share.

Loss of goodwill

Most of the goodwill loss in offshoring is due to negative publicity, which wanes after the press loses interest in the subject and the company becomes more efficient and profitable. Attention is then focused on positive aspects that offshore outsourcing brings to the company.

However, not offshoring can lead to the ultimate loss of goodwill— customer attrition. If no players in an industry send processes offshore, there is no threat to the loss of goodwill. However, even if a couple of players do go offshore, others have no option but to follow, just to be on a level playing field. These following two scenarios illustrate the problem.

Two tales of four companies

To illustrate the costs to companies not outsourcing, the following two examples describe two sets of two companies.

An R&D tale

Manufacturing Company A is in the plastics business, developing new compounds to create stronger materials. Due to a shortage of talent, it takes a long time to develop new products and get them to market. Its competition, Company B, has outsourced a lot of its R&D work to India, and the US team works with the Indian team to develop new plastic compounds.

The packaging industry has been demanding a new plastic product with higher tensile strength and the look and feel of glass. Company A is facing several problems by retaining R&D on-site. It needs a larger team to work on the project but is unable to find the talent locally and cost-effectively. It can afford to pay high salaries for a new team of R&D scientists but can't do so as it will affect the compensation parity in the company.

Company A also has to set up a larger facility for the project, even though the cost of real estate is high. R&D is a high-risk business, and the company does not know if it will ever be able to develop and patent the compound the market needs before its competition.

Company B has no problem recruiting chemical engineers in India. To meet the market demand for the new plastic compound, it hires a team of 50 engineers in 45 business days. Since Company B is a multinational organization, it is an employer of choice and is flooded with résumés a couple of hours after an online job posting. These engineers are much less expensive than any in the US.

With low-cost facilities in India, Company B quickly expands its R&D facility to house the 50 engineers. After putting the necessary technology in place, it commences R&D well before Company A, thereby increasing its chances of filing patents first.

After a few months, Company A hires engineers on-site, sets up the required infrastructure at a high cost, and starts R&D for the plastic compound. However, it falls further behind Company B each day due to its inefficiently structured execution process.

37

Company A engineers come to work at 9 am and work on their projects until 6 pm, thus stopping R&D every evening. However, at Company B, after its engineers finish the day in the US, for example, the work is handed over to engineers in India, and R&D never sleeps.

In a market where the demand for the new material is strong and it's vital to lock in patents, Company B has a better chance of winning. By going offshore, it has stayed ahead of Company A in hiring talent, building cost-effective facilities, and speeding up R&D. Company A faces the risk of losing the patent race and, ultimately, market share and goodwill.

A business processes tale

In a financial services company that does not offshore a call center or accounting process, the loss of goodwill may be gradual and noticed too late. Insurance Company C has decided to retain all its functions on-site, whereas Company D has offshored several functions, including claims processing and the call center associated with it.

Claims processing is dealing with a customer who has suffered a loss, so promptness on the part of employees is very important. Errors in claims processing or lack of knowledge about the subject can turn the customer off. This book has shown how processes transferred to an offshore center have better process quality.

Company D has an advantage over Company C: Its claims processing function is of higher quality because its offshore vendor gives the function the time and attention of a core process and makes improvements to it. And with the high degree of attrition in call centers in the US, it will be difficult for Company C to retain knowledge. It will spend a lot of time in training new recruits, and their level of error will be high, leading to loss of customers.

The danger for Company C is that its customers will leave one at a time, and the company will not even notice until too late. Fixing the broken process on-site will be expensive; transferring the process offshore when customer attrition is high is risky because of the time required and possible breakdowns during the transfer. The loss of goodwill is very high.

Chapter 4
The Offshore Progression

In *The Wealth of Nations*, Adam Smith illustrated efficiencies achieved through division of labor—the basic economic notion that labor resources are best used when work tasks are divided among different workers. This allows workers to specialize in production, as each becomes highly skilled at specific tasks. Division of labor is so fundamental to the economy that its importance is occasionally overlooked in the real world. It is this specialization that makes up for foreign trade, where countries produce goods and services they excel in and later exchange. Offshore outsourcing is simply the division of labor across national boundaries. The deep talent pool of specialized and cost-effective labor overseas and the immigration and minimum wage laws preventing its free flow into North America and Europe have led to a dramatic rise in offshore outsourcing.

Today, the offshoring market is populated by a host of global players, even though the whole thing started only about a decade ago. The tentative steps to offshore information technology processes began in 1994; business processes in 1997. For both, 1999 was the defining year, when numerous customers in North America started adopting the strategy. The early adopters were such top Fortune 500 companies as GE, Citibank, Wal-Mart, and Northwestern Mutual: Their success pushed other companies along the same path.

Outsourcing information technology

In information technology (IT), the need to start using enterprise resource planning (ERP) software packages prompted companies to look offshore to meet the talent shortfall of the mid to late 1990s. With most of the work executed by imported talent on-site in North America, this was the region's initial exposure to offshore services.

Offshore outsourcing got a major boost in the three years leading up to 2000. Fixing the Y2K bug put a strain on the limited US talent pool. Since most of the Y2K work involved testing and routine bug-fixing activity, the function was exported, with almost 80 percent of the solutions built and deployed from offshore development centers.

With the Internet boom, the demand for exotic Web technologies and the engineers to write net programs far exceeded the demand for ERP or Y2K professionals. Even though offshore vendors met most of the demand for Web programmers, projects were executed on-site. Only 30 to 40 percent of the work was done offshore.

Outsourcing application maintenance—largely routine and mission critical but non-core tasks of most organizations—started taking entire projects offshore in 2001.

Enterprise resource planning

In most companies, the different departments—finance, human resources (HR), sales, warehousing, and production—have their own customized computer systems built to meet their needs. ERP removes these stand-alone computer systems and replaces them with a unified software program. Departments still get their own software, but they are modules linked together to make the complete order fulfillment system visible to anyone in the company.

In a non-ERP environment, order fulfillment is a paper-based flow from department to department, as parts of the order are completed. During this journey, the order is re-keyed into the computer systems of different departments over and over again, resulting in delays and lost orders, not to mention keying errors, which make order tallying difficult. And since the computer systems of the different departments are not connected, no one in the company has an exact status of the order at any given time. There is no way that sales can get into the finance department's computer to check if the order has been billed or the warehouse's computer system to see whether the item has been shipped.

With ERP, people in different departments all see the same information and can update it. When one department finishes with the order, it is automatically routed via the ERP system to the next department. To find out where the order is at any time, users need only log in to the system and track it down. The order process moves rapidly through the organization, and customers get their orders faster, with fewer errors. The net result is substantial cost and time saving.

Shortly after its introduction, companies kept the ERP process on-site for a number of reasons. Getting departments, which were used to functioning independently, to work together could be problematic, requiring management attention. Since the concept of offshoring was new and structured global communication infrastructure was not in place, management was not willing to let go of the processes. And ERP also involved a depth of business logic: Corporations felt that communicating this logic across borders might lead to gaps, which could create programs running off flawed logic.

There are several reasons for implementing an ERP package, and a run through them will show the amount of business logic involved in building the software.

The integration of financial information is a key goal of an ERP package. In any company, finance has its own set of revenue numbers, sales has another version, and different business units have their own version of costing, some even refusing to add on costs to their books. The result is that top management does not get a complete view of the revenue and cost streams. Therefore, it has to apply strict business logic, which has to be conveyed accurately to the software engineer.

Standardizing HR information requires complex business logic to track employees' time and communicate with them about benefits and services.

ERP is a set of best practices for performing different functions. To get the most from the software, people inside the company must adapt their work methods to those outlined in the software. If ERP users don't agree that the work methods embedded in the software are better than the ones in use, they will resist change and demand that software be re-engineered to match the ways processes currently run. Implementing an ERP package and its extensive navigation through computer screens to record, retrieve, and clear transactions requires software consultants on-site to guide the customer.

At the implementation stage, ERP projects can turn into failures. Many times, companies give in to the wishes of powerful business interests in the company and customize the software, which makes it less stable and harder to maintain, thus requiring software engineers on-site to execute the changes. When ERP was first introduced, the trend was to customize the software to meet process needs and not to eliminate wasteful processes. Companies not taking the tough route of changing processes ended up having to retain expensive software consultants on-site.

In the ERP era, keeping processes on-site was adopted due to the intricate nature of the work and its proximity to core functions. It also involved pulling the whole organization together, breaking down departmental barriers, and extensively using business logic. Also, talent access and not cost was the prime driver in the ERP era. The result was importing offshore talent on-site to speedily execute ERP projects.

Y2K

"Y2K" invoked images of planes falling from the sky, trains colliding into each other, and information systems crashing. However, although the issue was critical, the risks were exaggerated, and the problem was a technical glitch that could be easily resolved. The Y2K bug could create problems with mission-critical systems, but its solution was relatively routine and non-core.

The Y2K problem arose because modern computer systems had inherited default conventions from the mainframe era, when it was common practice to encode the year as a two-digit field. Since workstations and PCs were initially built to augment mainframe systems and use their data, the two-digit field practice spread throughout computer systems worldwide. This convention would have caused problems at the turn of the century and beyond.

In addition to the two-digit year coding, distinct issues surrounded the use of the six-digit date representation, and still other risks arose from the calculation of the leap year. And just to make matters worse, January 1, 2000, fell on a Saturday. Problems caused by coding errors would not be discovered until the next regular working day, allowing enough time for the errors to inflict a great deal of damage.

The problem affected hardware, languages and compilers, operating systems, random-number generators and security services, database management systems, transaction processing systems, EDI and banking systems, spreadsheets, PBXs, phone systems, and more. Many North American corporations saw no value in retaining Y2K programmers on-site at high cost to fix the problem. Therefore, a lot of Y2K work was executed offshore.

By 1998, when Y2K bug-fixing activity reached its peak, the communication infrastructure had improved substantially. It enabled programmers located offshore to run tests and fix bugs remotely. Many companies continued to fix the bug on-site, but corporations that hired offshore vendors exported the process completely. These were the defining years for offshore vendors. They were recognized as excellent providers of low-value software solutions.

Unlike ERP, whose process touches every aspect of the organization as well as several core functions, Y2K fixing was a non-core routine task. Therefore, companies were much more willing to send it offshore.

E-commerce

E-commerce is basically doing business on the Internet. In the 1990s, e-commerce was associated with e-tailing, hyped by the likes of eBay and Amazon.com. But e-commerce is all the trade possibilities that can take place over the Internet between corporations and their customers and vendors. It was the business-to-business that was poised to gain the most from the Internet boom.

The boom in e-commerce in 1999 greatly increased the demand for software technologies. With a dearth of programmers available to create successful e-business platforms, programming costs soared. Still, companies preferred to develop software platforms on-site because an e-commerce strategy was core to the organization and the rapid pace at which new technologies were released gave no clear picture of the direction e-commerce would take. E-commerce touched organizations much more deeply than did ERP and dramatically increased their reach into the value chain, touching both their vendors and their customers—and organizations were aware that technology bugs could easily turn off customers. Given that e-commerce was so close to a company's revenue source, managers were not comfortable outsourcing it offshore.

There are several key components to a successful e-commerce strategy and consequent benefits. Its success is based on integration throughout the organization, which enables significant efficiencies. Companies that take advantage of these opportunities are better placed to expand their markets and outperform their rivals.

Companies executed e-commerce strategies to open up a communications channel with vendors and customers and gain visibility and greater control of their value chain. Their goals in going onto the World Wide Web were to gain: direct access to clients and suppliers; cost-effective extension of marketing and product reach; the ability to measure product interest through examination of user access to corporate Web sites; the ability to efficiently manage the entire sales process electronically, from purchase to fulfillment to billing; and better visibility and control of the total value chain.

As corporations rushed to realize their e-commerce goal, they realized that their software systems needed to be ramped up. Going online required: building interactive interfaces to deal with the needs of the customer; re-engineering internal information systems to present information residing deep in the company's databases to customers and vendors; handling privacy issues of customers; building a secure transactional channel to protect payments and financial information; extending the ERP infrastructure to the Internet; and extending the company to vendors and customers over a wireless infrastructure.

Several corporations adopted e-commerce to enable such functions as electronic ordering, tracking, and payment systems, which incorporated their supply chain to lower the cost of inventory and its management. The strategy was also aimed at improving cash flows through electronic payments and reporting outstanding account data and reducing back-office accounting costs by cutting manual tasks for processing orders, payments, and product inquiries. Better and more current reporting of sales and support performance through the availability of online reports across all business functions was another goal.

It was clear that executing an e-commerce strategy would touch an organization more deeply than ERP had ever done. As developing a software platform for e-commerce needed extensive co-ordination between the various departments of an organization as well as incorporation of complex business logic, corporations felt comfortable keeping the process on-site. In hindsight, however, the strategy was expensive and unnecessary. Today, a lot of Web development takes place offshore, given the excellent communication links and mature delivery processes; but in 1999, speed was crucial and corporations were unwilling to devote management time to work with an offshore delivery model.

As corporations broke down the pieces of executing a successful e-commerce strategy, they realized that the demands of technology were overwhelming:

- Ensuring security and privacy of data communications was necessary to increase the comfort of customers and vendors. Customers transmit important financial information over the Web, including credit card and social security numbers. Vendors, too, transfer bank account and routing numbers. It was crucial that this data be protected to prevent fraud by hackers or even employees in the corporation.

- Creating dynamic content was needed to give customers information to make a purchase decision, to track the order for the customer, to provide product catalogues based on previous purchases, and so on. Dynamic content generation runs off sophisticated algorithms and data-mining engines.

- Online payment capture and authorization was needed to complete the sales transaction. This involved securely connecting with the information systems of credit companies and banks. Banks play a crucial role in the selling process by facilitating payment authorization and settlement. Online payment reduces the cost of payments through lower transaction rates and reduction in labor costs associated with manual processing, as well as enabling real-time processing of payments. Also, by moving to electronic payment, e-commerce companies get accurate and timely reporting of cash flows, sales performance, and bad debts. Cash flows can also be improved due to the shorter settlement periods of electronic payment instruments over paper-based payments such as checks.

- The rapid growth of e-commerce meant that the back-end systems also had to grow to handle user requests. It also meant integration of their back-end and front-end systems.

Connectivity and scalability issues meant companies needed to work very closely with their software vendors.

Corporations decided to keep a major chunk of their e-commerce projects on-site. Why?

The accelerated rollout of an e-commerce strategy meant that all its elements had to be communicated effectively to the technology team. It meant freezing the business requirement that included identification of key projects and processes—existing business initiatives and areas that could benefit from the electronic re-engineering of their processes. It also meant defining long-term and immediate e-commerce needs and building the software architecture to meet them. All these functions needed close interaction with the technology team.

Companies also had to assess their capability in terms of people skills and technology infrastructure. They needed to identify their level of understanding of e-commerce tools and their applications and their ability to support e-commerce. As well, they had to link their e-commerce strategy to their technology strategies to ensure they gained tangible benefits from electronic business transactions with trading partners. This required an on-site software team.

Moving into e-commerce also meant that corporations had to assess the readiness of their customers and suppliers to use e-commerce to conduct business transactions. Therefore, one of the jobs of the technology teams was to evaluate the ability of trading partners' technology to collaborate virtually in the areas of marketing, finance, operations, supply chain, and administrative tasks.

Companies also had to evaluate the opportunities and threats posed by competitors' e-commerce systems and benchmark their own software platform to world-class standards. Therefore, the technology team had to study industry trends in software and incorporate cutting-edge solutions for its company. Given the rapid pace of new technologies, development in the e-commerce space and meeting the goal of an accelerated rollout of a robust platform would not have been possible with an offshore technology team.

Speed to market, rapidly evolving technologies, proximity to core operations, and the need for close interaction with the technology teams prompted companies to execute major portions of e-commerce platform development on-site. And as initial public offerings were made to raise money from the investors for funding e-commerce ventures, cost was not considered an issue.

Today, this work can be executed offshore, given the mature delivery processes and communications infrastructure. But in the business environment of the e-commerce boom, IT managers were uncomfortable giving up control to an offshore vendor.

Application maintenance outsourcing

Information technology connects companies—manufacturing, service, software—internally and externally. But complications arise from multiple hardware platforms; diverse application development environments; countless desktop packages; endless upgrades; complex multi-vendor problem, resolution, and helpdesk processes; network upgrades; and so on. Mastering these complexities is nearly impossible due to the number of elements that constantly change and the rate at which these changes occur.

The ever-changing IT environment poses great hardships for its users and developers. This has a profound impact on the corporate budgets because of the overheads incurred. Application management outsourcing (AMO) is the ultimate solution to these complex problems.

AMO is the strategic use of outside specialized, efficient service providers to perform major, repetitive, non-core functions traditionally handled by internal staff and resources. These are often specific development projects or even entire application maintenance work. Businesses have always contracted for shared access to software resources that are beyond their individual reach, be it development, maintenance, or networking.

By the year 2001, when the e-commerce boom was waning, AMO had begun to pick up.

AMO can be divided into three basic businesses models:

- Product outsourcing: The client organization contracts an external service provider to perform all or part of the functions of one or more of its process components. With large and complex systems, where the client organization does not have the capacity or required skill, developing a particular component is outsourced. Functions outsourced include new product development, new technologies that require extensive research and expertise, and software management processes like design, code building, and testing.

- Product re-engineering: The client organization contracts an external service provider to perform all or part of the functions of one or more of the process steps involved in changing an existing software component, through feature enhancements or modifications, new technology migration, code optimization, performance tuning, and new operating system support.

- Production support: The client organization contracts an external service provider to perform every activity associated with software maintenance and support, including design, development, code building, testing, and maintenance. A clearly drafted service level agreement governs and guides the collaboration. Typically, organizations spend over 50 percent of their IT budget maintaining old software. When software resources are expended on maintenance, economic constraints and lack of sufficient technical personnel limit the development of new systems. This is one of the main reasons why many Fortune 500 companies outsource production support functions.

AMO is growing at a rapid pace. Fueled by slow economic growth and a desire to cut IT costs without sacrificing new development, chief information officers are exploring the use of global resources more than ever. According to the International Data Corporation, US-based companies alone will more than triple their application outsourcing spending from $5.5 billion in 2000 to more than $17.6 billion in 2005. Forrester Research predicts that the amount of IT budgets going offshore will more than double by 2003 to 28 percent.

As application management is routine and non-core, corporations are willing to export the functions offshore. Moving the process offshore frees up resources and cash that can be invested in core tasks.

Outsourcing business processes

Business process outsourcing (BPO) is the export of an entire business process, such as accounting, payroll, or logistics, to a vendor. Offshore BPO initially went to Ireland, but India has emerged as the leader—employing nearly 110,000 people and earning revenues of $1.5 billion in 2001–2002. Most offshore BPO has its roots in IT outsourcing, with players like Infosys Technologies and Wipro Technologies leveraging their IT experience to move into the BPO space. Customers are comfortable outsourcing business processes to their IT vendors, having worked with them for over half a decade.

There is a key distinction between IT and BPO. IT outsourcing lowers costs and introduces new efficiencies through the use of advanced technologies; however, IT vendors are not responsible for accomplishing the business results. They will, for instance, provide cutting-edge accounting software but will not perform the actual accounting. In BPO, the vendor assumes the complete operational and strategic responsibility of a function such as HR or finance and accounting. Cost savings are the prime driver to outsource offshore, but customers gain such crucial benefits as quality, process improvements, increased return on investments, and the ability to allocate resources to core functions. In effect, the BPO vendor takes responsibility for the ownership, administration, execution, and results of that process.

Overview

For several years, North American and European companies have been outsourcing such functions as customer relationship management (CRM), HR, and finance and accounting to local companies. Many US corporations have been outsourcing payroll functions to companies like Ceridian and ADP, and several vendors also provide call center services. After 1997, many of these functions were being exported offshore, a strategy that has delivered value; provided innovative services; accelerated change; taken the burden of investing in people, processes, and technology off balance sheet; and given best-in-class processes.

Companies like Wal-Mart, GE, and Conseco looked at Microsoft and Oracle exporting their core software development tasks and getting benefits, and saw no reason to retain their own non-core call centers or billing processes on-site. Once companies accept that non-core processes need not be retained on-site, they begin to outsource low-value processes. When they feel comfortable, they outsource functions of greater value and those supporting strategic directions and initiatives. This creates higher value due to the scale of operations.

Industry surveys show that companies will significantly ramp up BPO. Market research firm Gartner discovered that about five percent of US corporations with revenues of $100 million to $4 billion outsourced or plan to outsource back-office functions offshore. Gartner has pegged the global market for business process outsourcing at $178 billion by 2005.

Once companies realize the cost and quality benefits of BPO, the ramp-up is rapid. GE had a target of 10,000 people for its Indian BPO arm GECIS by 2005; however, the demand for the services of GECIS resulted in the number of employees touching nearly 11,000 by mid-2003.

Along with the increasing number of companies moving offshore, the number of functions outsourced is growing. On the software and IT front, companies that have been outsourcing testing and maintenance functions are transferring more complex functions like customer support, product development, and R&D offshore.

The BPO offshoring trend began with basic functions like medical transcriptions and outbound call centers and moved up the value chain in offering engineering design services and credit card billing. Large transnational corporations like Citibank set up their own captive service centers in India. These were labor-intensive operations that involved the conversion of data from paper to a digitized form, basically transforming data into information and then into knowledge that could support managerial decision making. As information in the systems grew, so did the need for an educated workforce. But that resulted in an increase in costs and also the need to hire in greater number. These two factors fed each other, dramatically pushing up the cost for corporations. Therefore, several corporations decided to move these functions to more cost-effective domains.

To handle back-office work, HSBC has an office in India, which employs over 1,200 workers, and has plans to expand. British

Airways has moved many of its financial and accounting functions to its offshore offices in India, while America Online's customer service operations are supported from India. The effort-based cost savings, which just looks at the cost of labor, is as high as 75 percent. Cost savings on a transactional basis is about 50 percent.

Data entry and data conversion services are fairly simple processes far removed from the core. These can involve anything from medical transcriptions to digitization of paper documents. The work volume in data services is very high, and the number of people employed in it substantial. The data are stored in relational databases and retrieved by the client machines anywhere in the world. The data in their native format are shipped physically to the vendors, where transformation takes place. Once converted to an electronic form, porting back to the client's system is easy. GE ships a lot of documents to Mexico for digitization.

But some core functions are moving out, too. For instance, another leading player that plans to ship data entry offshore is Reuters, the UK-based wire service news agency. The content function, which generates the financial data Reuters sells to banks and other key customers, will be shipped to India. This will affect the staff of 350 based in Tiverton in southwest England, another 65 in Edinburgh in Scotland, as well as a further 600 in New York and White Plains in the US, Singapore in East Asia, and in several other offices around the world. This is a core function for Reuters, as the company makes most of its money from financial data it sells rather than from selling news to papers and broadcasters. Reuters is in the middle of a 3,000-staff redundancy and cost-cutting program.

Non-core, or contextual, processes are the easiest part of the business to outsource, especially non-critical ones like facility management or cafeteria services. But even critical and non-core functions like HR administration, call center operations, and accounting are getting outsourced today.

Long-distance phone service companies have a typical process for deciding if a task is core or context. Before selling a long-distance phone service to a customer, a company will check their credit history and any prior relationships with it. Before making offers to about 100 potential customers with similar profiles, the company will filter out at least 1,000 other people. These are back-end processes and contextual to the core activity of selling the phone service. There are other processes much further away from the core, like acquiring the list of 1,000 names with their current long-distance service provider.

As the vendor gains experience and improves service quality with process specialization, functions closer to core get offshored. GE runs a BPO company in India, GE Capital International Services (GECIS), to offshore in-house processes cost-effectively and to improve process quality. GECIS, which began with data entry processes that are far from the core, moved closer by exporting contact center, accounting, technology helpdesk, and engineering design functions.

Outsourced business processes can be broadly classified into contact service operations, data functions and high-impact R&D, and stock research. Contact functions cover customer interaction services, including call centers and e-mail support.

Contact services

Contact services form a large chunk of BPO offshoring. India alone employs 33,000 people in them, with revenues of nearly $375 million in 2001–2002. Call center functions get closer to core processes as the offshore vendor interacts with the client's customers. This customer contact point can result in loss of clients if the vendor's processes are not mature. The two-way information transfer between the client's customer and the vendor has to be painless. Recently, long-distance telephone service companies lost customers when vendors provided incorrect rates, quoting low phone rates to win new customers and then charging them at a higher rate in the bill.

The vendor is usually just a channel to transfer highly structured and telemarketing information over international phone lines. Contact centers also respond to inbound calls from customers concerning a variety of issues. Vendors contact their client's customer to collect delinquent payments, initiating balance transfer transactions, cross-selling, or up-selling products. They not only can draw information from their client's system to perform these tasks but also have write-access to its database and can update information by entering the details and outcome of any interactions with the end client. Often, the vendor will have a backup, or mirror, database, which is synchronized live or as a batch process. Other contact center services include e-mail support or live online support, where the vendor responds to a client's customer through e-mail or an online messenger.

Amazon.com has outsourced both call center and e-mail services to Daksh, India, to provide expanded customer service around the clock. Amazon.com has seven customer service locations in the US, Netherlands, UK, and Germany. Service center staff members answer questions about specific orders or about the company's Web site in general. Amazon.com works closely with Daksh eServices to ensure a seamless experience for its customers. Its goal is to increase company profits, as the labor costs in India are far less than those in the US. As cost becomes a driving factor, Amazon.com will outsource more work to India. Many companies quickly ramp up offshore operations to gain cost efficiencies, quality processes, and talent access, including GE and the Dutch bank ABN AMRO.

Some functions in contact services involve problem solving. This needs a higher level of judgment on the part of the vendor's employees, who must judge if a course of action is according to the client's policies. For example, the BPO service provider's employee decides whether a business user of a long-distance telephone service plan can be switched in the middle of a contract period to retain business or if the service provider should make the decision. In most cases, vendors have enough information about the client's customers to resolve disputes based on broad policy guidelines. Here, the vendor has the discretion to make that decision. In the early stages of the offshoring exercise, most vendors reverted to the client for feedback. However, as the processes mature at the vendor's site, problems are solved without recourse to the client.

Rule-based support is much simpler, as it uses a set of rules supplied by the client to create solutions for its customers. The vendors use expertise gained at the job, information, and analytical skills with the client's rules for such tasks as providing technical support, enhancing credit limits, or approving insurance claims over the phone or Internet. Some rule-based support processes have low strategic impact on the core process of the organization; others are so close to the core that they can greatly affect the business.

Rule-based support for such processes as technical support and customer service clearly falls in the low-impact category. Failure in these processes usually does not disrupt core function in an organization, so they are the first to be exported. Since the quality, customer satisfaction levels, objectives, and risk for these processes are clearly measurable, companies are more comfortable exporting these low-impact functions to an offshore vendor.

Data functions

Data functions include back-office operations, revenue accounting, data entry, data conversion, finance and accounting, and HR services. Other data services include medical transcription and translation functions, content development, and animation.

Human resources

Although HR is mission critical, it does not provide a competitive edge to a company and so can easily be outsourced. Outsourcing involves engaging a service provider to manage the people, processes, and technologies related to a company's HR functions, such as payroll, benefits administration, training, recruitment, employee relationship management, relocation, expense management, travel, and HR management information systems. Given the costs and time involved in running an HR function in-house, several companies are offshoring it to reduce costs and improve service quality.

To service employees, the vendor may place an account manager on-site, as well as provide a toll-free number to answer questions about payroll and benefits. The vendor can also solve problems for employees if the solution is within a set of parameters, thus taking away a lot of day-to-day decision making from the company.

The vendor also manages compliance and liability issues by ensuring adherence to state and federal laws—hiring and terminating employees as per the law, updating employee handbooks, and adopting affirmative action programs. The vendor can also manage a lot of the paperwork HR administration generates, including personnel forms, policies, procedures, performance management records, and compensation records.

Under benefits management, the vendor imports: reconciling billing, implementing new benefit packages, answering employee queries, processing medical claims, and training employees from the customers site. It also handles such payroll functions as keying in data, including mandatory and voluntary withholdings; processes direct deposit, bonuses, commissions, and manual checks; and looks after payroll tax payments and W-2 statements and churning out payroll reports.

Most recruiting processes can be run remotely from offshore locations, including job postings, interviewing, reference checks, background checks, and drug tests. The same is true of training and development, where offshore vendors architect program design and delivery and set up training sessions for both HR and core businesses of the company.

Financial processes

Outsourcing financial services transfers non-core finance functions from the books of the company to a vendor offshore. Through remote connectivity to the customer's systems, the vendor typically executes accounts payable, accounts receivable, bank reconciliation, fixed asset management, employee expense reimbursement, general ledger maintenance, and management reporting.

A company outsourcing its accounting function offshore does so on a large scale, transferring about 100 to 500 full-time jobs. Pricing is generally on a cost-plus basis, with the vendor committed to bringing down costs through increased efficiencies.

High-impact processes

Management reporting, profit and cost center analysis, remote financial and accounting services, and R&D have a very high impact on the core processes, directly affecting a firm's strategic objectives. These functions are the last to be outsourced. Some firms are comfortable exporting the processes to a captive facility: GE Plastics has exported R&D to an in-house facility in India.

The results from these processes can have an immediate impact on a firm's core business strategy. If the Indian R&D center of GE Plastics discovers a new compound with the strength of steel, the sales and production strategies of the organization will change drastically. This kind of outsourcing is justified by the superior skill sets available at the GE Plastics India unit and the specialization that the R&D center enjoys.

Another high-impact process recently outsourced is stock research. The investment bank Lehman Brothers has outsourced stock research to Indian analysts. Since almost all the raw data needed for stock analysis are online, this function can be performed anywhere in the globe. When companies have analyst conferences, the analysts in India can attend virtually through Webcasts or conference calls.

Conclusion

Corporations worldwide are accepting the concept of offshore outsourcing with its benefits of cost, scale, speed, and quality. The number of robust independent local and multinational vendors offering services is the measure of its success. The offshore advantage is underscored by the fact that companies such as GE, Microsoft, Citibank, and British Airways have set up captive offshore service centers.

But the concept of cross-border division of labor took time to catch on. During the ERP boom, most of the work was kept on-site due to the intricate nature of the work and its proximity to core functions. ERP also needed the management push to get the entire organization together and break down departmental barriers. Later, as e-commerce touched an organization more deeply than ERP, companies tended to retain their technology development on-site. The speed to market of rapidly evolving technologies combined with the availability of cash prevented processes from going offshore.

However, when processes were not close to the core, as with Y2K and application maintenance, companies were comfortable sending them offshore. The trend to offshore gained momentum after the technology bust in 2001. With the economic slowdown, the cost factor came strongly into play, which, combined with the offshore success stories, led to several publicized deals in 2000 and 2001. And with proven successes, corporations were willing to offshore almost any software function.

As software offshoring grew and businesses saw its benefits, they began offshoring back-office functions. Offshore software service providers with their proven global delivery models moved into the space and set up shop to provide BPO. In the late 1990s, British Airways started sending business processes to India. Today, several vendors provide BPO from India and Ireland in the areas of transactional processing.

Offshoring is rapidly moving up the value chain. In the IT space, initially only low-value functions such as Y2K testing were sent offshore. Now companies like Microsoft and Oracle send core product development functions offshore. In the BPO space, vendors have moved up from providing contact services to high-end R&D. GE's technology center provides R&D services in the areas of aircraft engines and power systems.

Chapter 5
Multiple Delivery Channels, Varying Benefits

Offshoring solutions for the IT and BPO spaces can be delivered in various ways. IT tasks are executed at the client's site or completely offshore or divided between offshore and on-site locations. Sometimes the work is executed by offshore vendors at a location close to the customer or is distributed among several development centers. In the BPO space, 100 percent of the work is done offshore. There is a fundamental difference between the delivery model of software development and BPO. In the former, globally scattered teams interact on a regular basis as they work on an on-going project. This interaction is not needed in a call center, as the vendor's employees anywhere can access client data from a central database. This can be updated, and another representative can respond to the same customer, pulling the fresh information.

The three delivery modes—offshore, on-site, and blended—are used to execute consulting solutions, systems integration, application development, R&D, production support, and maintenance in the IT space.

In an offshore project, most functions are executed overseas. A small team of developers and a project manager may be based at the client site for IT projects; their role is to architect solutions after interacting with the client and handling relationship management issues. The offshore model is ideal for long-term or high-budget projects.

In an on-site project—ideal for short-term projects—the project team, led by a project manager, completes all the development work at the client site. Development can also take place at any of the vendor's offices located near the client site.

In a mixed-mode delivery, development takes place simultaneously at the customer site and at local and offshore development centers. A state-of-the-art communications infrastructure enables seamless and real-time tracking and co-ordination of projects. Offshore vendors have finely tuned the delivery mechanism, which gives customers the feel of on-site development. Mixed-mode delivery offers advantages of both offshore and on-site development, but it is more expensive than pure offshore development.

Offshore delivery

Offshore facilities in India and the Philippines give companies access to an effective alternative to traditional on-site development. With today's IT resource constraints, space constraints, and application development and customization requirements, using offshore facilities produces desired results at a fraction of on-site development costs.

Vendors operate state-of-the-art development facilities, fully equipped with hardware and software. They use local project and account management and offshore technical expertise. In BPO, most of the work is executed offshore, and few of the vendors' employees—perhaps a project manager, high-level programmers, and/or a relationship manager—are based at the client's site.

Offshore outsourcing greatly speeds development. The time zone difference allows companies to run 16 to 24 hours of programming a day without paying overtime. Two teams working in co-ordination in the US and India means more time spent on developing, testing, and launching software. The continuous workflow also reduces overall cost.

Although speed and availability of quality resources are compelling reasons to ship projects overseas, the most popular benefit of offshore outsourcing is its low cost. When faced with paying half as much for overall development on multi-million dollar projects, a company has a clear choice.

In an offshore project, vendors put in place version-control processes, co-ordinated through a quality-assurance manager. A project manager is based at the client site to overcome cultural barriers and facilitate communication with offshore programmers; a network manager at the vendor's site co-ordinates the logistics of using several communications providers across the continents. However, despite all the communication advances, the client still feels a loss of control over the project.

On-site delivery

On-site delivery offers clients technical IT expertise and project management in the form of staff augmentation and/or project-based engagements at the client's site. This is the most expensive form of delivery, as customers have to pay high local rates. The payment terms for on-site delivery would be on a time-and-materials fixed-bid basis.

Clients import software engineers on temporary work visas to execute the full project at their own site. Once the projects are over, the engineers return home. This mode of delivery is on the wane in the IT space and is not used by offshore vendors in the BPO arena.

Mixed-mode delivery

Mixed-mode delivery combines the benefits of on-site and offshore development. It integrates all the client locations involved in decision making, development, and support with all the vendors' own centers using a state-of-the-art communication infrastructure. This allows for a true 24/7 operation with the benefits of lower cost. To ensure seamless project co-ordination, vendors assign key resources—project managers, project architect, and lead project engineers—to all distributed projects at all the development centers.

Distributed development teams have established procedures for periodic reviews to identify project gaps at different development centers. They provide project status to the project managers and identify actions needed to move forward. These reviews are key for the successful 24-hour operation in distributed development.

R&D outsourcing is another function that works in the mixed mode. Scientists work in different time zones on the same development project. The work is divided over different geographic locations and is executed concurrently.

Partnership models

Staffing: Vendors provide staff for IT projects to meet resource gaps in BPO or software projects. Such models are extremely short term to meet surge requirements. Most companies have a list of preferred vendors that supply the resources

Project specific: A vendor is hired to implement a specific project either at offshore centers or the client's location. These can be very long-term relationships if they relate to IT development projects, business process outsourcing, or application maintenance outsourcing.

Build, operate, and transfer: In this model, the client asks the vendor to build offshore facilities to provide business process or IT development and maintenance facilities. Once the center is built, has operated for a few years and is stabilized, ownership is transferred to the client. The benefit is that the client gets the required expertise before taking over the offshore center.

Joint ventures: This is similar to the build, operate, and transfer model, but the ownership lies jointly with the vendor and client. With joint ventures, the client has a greater say in the management of the offshore center.

Conclusion

Of the three delivery modes, offshore delivery is the most favored, with its cost, scale, and speed advantages. In the BPO space, attempting a mixed-mode or on-site delivery takes away the purpose of exporting processes to an offshore vendor, which is cost-effective service delivery. Over the years, offshore vendors have been able to improve their delivery processes, making the quality of their work much better than that on-site. Most on-site outsourcing companies, including IBM Global Services, and EDS, are setting up offshore development centers to bring the benefits to this delivery model to their customers. The processes going offshore and the number of vendors providing services are growing at a brisk pace.

Chapter 6
The Market Players

Offshore players fall into three broad categories: independent local service providers, independent multinational service providers, and captive service providers.

Independent local service providers

Independent local service providers are owned locally—by Indian or Russian or Chinese investors—and have a majority of operations within their countries. The vendors have some sales presence and software consultants working in North America or Europe, but most of the work is executed offshore.

In India alone, there are over 800 IT vendors, with a few top companies firmly established in the global market. Even though their primary listing is on an Indian stock exchange, some companies are traded on international stock exchanges like the NASDAQ or the Luxembourg Stock Exchange. Most of these vendors have transparent accounting standards that adhere to US generally acceptable accounting practices. They also make constant improvements in the global delivery process, for which the Carnegie Mellon has assessed them at various SEI CMM levels.

Most local IT vendors leverage customer relationships to provide them with BPO services. Although there are over 150 independent BPO service providers based in India, only the ones launched by IT companies and captive players like GE have made a strong impact in the market. There are few independent service providers that are successful albeit not on the scale of Progeon, a subsidiary of Infosys Technologies, or Wipro Technologies' Spectramind. The BPO and IT market is expected to go through more consolidation, and the number of vendors will decrease. A look at few of the key players will give a clearer idea of the market space.

TCS and Intelenet

Tata Consultancy Services (TCS) is India's largest IT service provider, with total revenues of $1.04 billion for the year ending March 31, 2003. TCS services clients in over 55 countries through over 100 branches employing nearly 20,000 software consultants. It provides IT and business consulting services to governments, businesses, and industry—in finance and banking, insurance,

69

telecommunications, transportation, retail, manufacturing, pharmaceuticals, and utilities—in India and abroad.

TCS delivers its IT solutions from nine development centers in India alone, Budapest, Melbourne, New Jersey, Phoenix, Columbus, Huangzhou, and Yokohama. Its size enables it to provide cost-effective services to customers overseas and to stay profitable despite quoting one of the lowest rates in the industry.

After establishing a strong presence in the IT market, TCS moved to leverage the emerging opportunities in the BPO section, doing work for mutual funds and banks in back-office processing and inter-bank reconciliation. To move into the BPO space, TCS formed Intelenet Global Services as a joint venture with Housing Development Finance Corporation (HDFC) to deliver solutions to US, UK, and Canadian markets. TCS brought to the joint venture experience in executing and maintaining mission-critical projects, a technology implementation process, domain knowledge, and strong project-management skills, as well as an existing customer base. HDFC brought its experience in customer-management processes, back-office operations and property management in banking, insurance, mutual funds, asset management, and mortgage and properties.

Infosys

Infosys Technologies is a $753 million (revenues on March 31, 2003) consulting and IT services company with over 17,000 employees worldwide. It uses a low-risk global delivery model to accelerate schedules with a high degree of time and cost predictability.

Infosys works with large global corporations and new-generation technology companies to build new products or services and to implement prudent business and technology strategies. Its clients include Airbus, Boeing, ING Group, Microsoft, Nortel Networks, and Lucent. Infosys has a presence in Canada, the US, Argentina, Belgium, France, Germany, Sweden, Switzerland, the UK, UAE, India, China, Japan, Singapore, and Australia. For more information on Infosys, see "The Infosys Progeon story".

Wipro

Wipro Infotech provides global technology services. Listed on the New York Stock Exchange, it was ranked by *Business Week* in 2002 as the seventh largest software services company in the world. Through its 30 offices worldwide staffed by 13,000 software consultants, it services such clients as Boeing, Ericsson, Toshiba, Cisco, Seagate, Putnam Investments, United Technologies, Best Buy, IBM, Microsoft, NCR, Thames Water, Transco, and Sony.

Wipro provides IT consulting and product design services. IT consulting includes systems integration, package implementation, application development and maintenance, IT infrastructure outsourcing, and total outsourcing. Wipro has provided product design outsourcing to Microsoft, Epson, Magneti Marelli, NCR, Sony, and IBM, among others.

Wipro did not provide BPO until 2002 when it acquired Spectramind, a start-up company that offered a range of remote processing applications, including customer interaction services, business process outsourcing, and knowledge services. By entering the market through an acquisition, Wipro Spectramind benefited from an existing customer base.

iGATE

iGATE Corporation is a $292 million, Pittsburgh-based holding company of a group of software services companies with offshore development centers in Canada, India, and China, and on-site development centers in Pittsburgh. It has over 4,000 employees and is listed on the NASDAQ.

Its subsidiary iGATE Global Solutions is publicly listed in India, where it provides outsourced IT services from both on-site/onshore and offshore locations from eight global development centers. iGATE Mastech Professional Services offers clients staffing and IT training services—on-site, co-managed, value-based, and permanent placement services. The company also provides a complete suite of Web-based, instructor-led learning programs for customers worldwide. iGATE Global Process Outsourcing is the BPO subsidiary.

iGATE Clinical Research International offers a complete range of site management support services for conducting Phase I–IV clinical trials in the US, India, and other countries. To enter the clinical trials space, iGATE had acquired PCRN (Pittsburgh Clinical Research Network) and DiagnoSearch (Mumbai), which together had conducted over 200 clinical trials in a number of therapeutic areas.

Mascon

Mascon, a global IT services company, saw 2002–2003 revenues of $60 million. Recognized as the fastest growing technology company in Chicago by Deloitte Touche Tohmatsu for 2002, Mascon provides end-to-end solutions based on an offshore and onshore delivery model. The company's shares are listed on the stock exchanges of Luxembourg in Europe and Mumbai, Chennai, New Delhi, and Jaipur in India.

Mascon has 1,200 professionals in development centers in India, the US, the UK, Latin America, and Canada, providing vertical solutions across financial services (banking and insurance), telecom, retail and distribution, manufacturing, and academia, with capabilities across horizontal solutions in consulting, enterprise systems, enterprise applications, systems integration, and e-business. Its clients include Citibank, GE, Eastman Kodak, and Walgreen. For more information on Mascon, see "The Mascon story".

MphasiS

The MphasiS Group provides offshore services in IT and BPO. MsourcE provides value-added contact center and BPO services for Fortune 500 companies from English-language delivery centers in Bangalore and Pune, India, and a Spanish-language facility in Tijuana, Mexico. It implements integrated contact centers that converge all the media of customer contact points, thus providing a complete suite of services to its clients. MphasiS BFL designs, builds, and maintains information technology architecture and applications for Fortune 500 companies in financial services, technology, and logistics. Services cover the spectrum from IT architecture and system integration to application development.

This India-based company has offshore development centers and is listed on Indian stock exchange.

Daksh

Daksh, a typical independent start-up funded by venture capital, offers only BPO services. Its cost-effective integrated customer care services include e-mail responses, real-time chat, call center services, knowledge management, customized customer relation management architecture, and related value-added services.

Daksh has based its business development, customer interface, and consulting function in the US and delivers service from New Delhi, India. The company serves five areas: e-commerce and retail, telecommunications, banking, financial services and insurance, travel, and high technology. Its capabilities are structured to provide voice and data services for both US and UK English.

Several smaller companies in India are struggling to survive; however, Daksh has been is one of the successful start-up BPO companies, due both to its strong client list, which includes Amazon.com and Yahoo, and to venture capital funding.

V6 Technologies

V6 Technologies is a Russian software company formed in 1996 to offer offshore services in Web applications, business-to-business and business-to-consumer systems, search engines, intranet solutions, catalogues, and large corporate portals. Its operations include J2EE and Microsoft.NET. Software development uses advanced architecture design, multi-tier solutions, and open object-oriented programming. It employs specialists certified by Sun, Microsoft, Oracle, IBM, and Hewlett-Packard. It caters to international customers based in the UK, France, the US, Israel, and Austria.

Software Ventures International

Software Ventures International (SVI), a Philippines-based offshore service provider, was formed in 1986. SVI and its subsidiaries provide an array of IT, contact center, and BPO services. SVI focuses on the international marketplace with such clients as Morgan Stanley, Safeway, and Northwest Airlines. In 2000, SVI acquired Telemarketing Concepts (TCI) to gain entry into the call center space, with in-bound customer support, human resources support, technical support, and outbound telemarketing. Its other BPO services include back-office processing, medical transcription, litigation support, and broadcast media monitoring.

Independent multinational service providers

Multinational service providers have established service centers in such countries as India and China to leverage the cost benefits of offshore delivery. Like the local service providers, these companies cater to needs of outside customers.

Companies like EDS and IBM Global Services have established bases in India to protect their customer base from penetration by the independent local service providers. Local service providers offer better value since multinational service providers have to load the cost of their large and expensive US or European operations onto their price. However, existing customer relationships result in large offshoring deals going to the multinationals.

EDS

Electronic Data Systems (EDS), founded in 1962, is the leading global information technology service company. EDS employs 138,000 people in 60 countries and serves more than 35,000 business and government clients around the world. Its revenues were $21.5 billion in 2001, with over 40 percent coming from outside the US. EDS provides application services, BPO, business and technology consulting, EAI/Web services, hosting services, and supply chain management.

Spurred by the technological boom and regulatory reforms of the mid-1990s, EDS entered India in 1996. It provides cost-effective services to EDS's global accounts by leveraging the local talent pool, high-speed data communication, and the time zone difference to create a virtual, 24-hour office. EDS India also services the domestic market along with its independent subsidiary, A.T. Kearney. EDS India was the first company in India to sign a multi-year outsourcing contract with global customer General Motors India. It now has three facilities in India, offering systems development, management, support and integration, data center and network management, business process management, and management consulting.

IBM

IBM Global Services provides IT support to its customers worldwide from its India operations. IBM entered India to leverage its cost-effective delivery model and deep talent pool. IBM provides the people, processes, and tools to maintain the IT infrastructure of its customers, supporting hardware, operating system, and networking for a wide range of IBM and non-IBM platforms. IBM Global's customized support services assist a company's IT organization by taking on all or selected operational tasks. Taking the support from its offshore resources in India, IBM provides application management services, e-business hosting, integrated technology services, network services, security and privacy services, storage services, strategic outsourcing, and wireless services. IBM product support's offering includes preventive maintenance for key systems and peripherals, on-site and carry-in repair facilities, customization of service window and service levels, software handholding, migration, fixes, system recovery, and performance tuning.

IBM's scale of operations is huge. To meet its customer's requirements, it sources talent from second-tier local software companies. After sourcing talent from other players in the market, IBM marks up the rate and supplies the software engineers to the end customer. As in most multinational software companies, the rates of IBM Global's services are higher than those of its local Indian counterparts. But existing relationships and the ability to scale are the factors that retain clients.

Captive service providers

Captive service providers are units of North American or European corporations that have set up shop in offshore locations. These units have no local ownership and cater solely to providing services for the parent and group companies.

GE has a host of facilities that cater to BPO, IT, and R&D needs of all units. Microsoft has a cutting-edge technology center in India to develop new software for global markets. ABN AMRO Bank and Citibank have BPO facilities, which serve their worldwide operations.

Microsoft

In 1998, Microsoft set up its India Development Center to develop new products cost-effectively. In the meantime, Microsoft is investing $400 million over three years beginning in 2002 for education, partnerships, innovation, and localization of IT, a major chunk of which will go to the center.

The center has a group that is responsible for developing new technologies in enterprise storage management, including NAS, data protection, and multi-site high-availability products. Enterprise storage is a major focus area for Microsoft, and the center plays a critical role in driving the strategy and developing new technologies for this space.

The development center was also responsible for developing a complete software product for the global market, Visual J#.Net, a development tool that enables Java language developers to build applications and services on its .NET framework.

Microsoft's India presence is giving it unprecedented access to a cost-effective talent pool, placing Microsoft on the cutting edge in the global marketplace.

GE

GE is the largest offshore outsourcer to India and China, with projected annualized savings of $1 billion by 2005 from India. Its captive centers provide specialized services to GE's units overseas, as well as to some units outside the GE umbrella. Offshore services include BPO, software engineering, and R&D. GE exported these functions for the same reasons other companies do—cost-effective access to a deep talent pool.

GE Capital Services offers offshore outsourcing services through several individual entities. By offering internal and external clients the opportunity to outsource non-core processes, GE Capital enables them to focus resources on key aspects of their business.

GE Software Solutions provides services in the technology domains of Oracle applications and Siebel, including implementation, development, transition, maintenance and support, and upgrades. GE Capital Integrated Business Solutions focuses on building global business platforms, IT-enabled services, and product-specific solutions. iProcess provides IT-enabled business process outsourcing services, such as helpdesk services and a range of e-commerce fulfillment services, including Web-based customer service. And finally, under GE Capital, the Analytics Center of Excellence (ACoE) provides modeling and analytics support to GE capital businesses. By providing data-driven business strategies to a variety of functional areas like asset management, collections, fraud, marketing, pricing, and risk, ACoE improves processes and profitability of GE units.

The John F. Welch Technology Center in Bangalore, India, is a multi-disciplinary R&D center, assisting GE's R&D capabilities to bring new technologies faster to the market. It collaborates with GE's two other R&D facilities in Schenectady, NY, and Shanghai, China, which form the GE Global Research team, to conduct research, development, and engineering activities for GE's diverse businesses worldwide. The technology center also conducts R&D for several other GE businesses.

To read about the full extent of GE's offshoring activities, see "The GE Story".

Conclusion

Ownership of offshore service providers is clearly differentiated, but the services they provide are not. Most independent providers offer services similar in terms of price, speed, and quality. Awarding a contract to a specific vendor comes down to price or a pre-existing relationship.

This market space sees competition between local and multinational service providers. Local vendors try to differentiate themselves in quality, scale, domain expertise, and speed to market, but in reality, any of the top service providers can meet all these deliverables. The top players have over 8,000 employees, which gives them the scale. All the top players are SEI CMM level 5 assessed, which ensures quality processes, and all of them tap from the same talent pool. The scale and the quality processes combined with the benefit of time zone difference gives all the top local vendors the requisite speed to execute projects.

The same may not be true of tier-II vendors. These vendors may not have the scale and domain expertise that the top-level players have. They may be certified for quality, but their operations are much smaller, and top talent is absorbed by the top local players and multinational vendors. However, the smaller vendors make up for these shortcomings by offering flexibility and individual attention to customers. Their contracts often give customers a lot of management control on the project-execution processes. And because their client portfolio is small, tier-II players can give top management time to their customers.

Multinational vendors like EDS and IBM have the international experience of exporting large-scale projects involving over 1,000 people at a time. These vendors, however, lose out on price as they load the cost of their North American and European operations. But multinational vendors win contracts by leveraging existing relationships.

Captive service providers like GE or Microsoft India do not compete in the market for customers. However, they compete in the local market for the same talent. Captive service providers have the task of selling their offerings within the company.

Chapter 7
The Country Advantage

Chapter 7
The Country Advantage

In moving IT and business processes offshore, a company must choose which country it wants to outsource to, most likely India, Russia, China, the Philippines, or Ireland. This involves evaluating such factors as geopolitical risks, knowledge domain strengths, talent pool, comparative costs, and work culture.

India—a clear winner, for now

For cost and quality, India is the best country to outsource IT and business processes to. Indeed, 90 percent of the software processes offshored land in India, which has emerged as the leader in the BPO space. As well, it has a very stable business and political climate. Even during times of political change, business has not been affected.

India also has the largest population of skilled IT labor. The National Association of Software and Service Companies (NASSCOM) states that India has 4.3 million technical workers, of whom 250,000 are in software services. The country produces nearly 73,500 software professionals annually and is expected to bridge a major part of the gap in IT talent in the US.

Nearly 19 million students are enrolled in high schools and 10 million students in pre-graduate degree courses across India. Moreover, 2.1 million graduates and 0.3 million post-graduates emerge from India's non-engineering colleges. By 2008, there will be about 17 million people available to the IT industry. The Indian education system emphasizes mathematics and science, resulting in a large number of science and engineering graduates. With their proficient English, they have enabled the country to take advantage of the international demand for IT talent.

India has three types of training organizations: educational institutions run and funded by the government; privately-owned polytechnics recognized by software leaders like Microsoft and IBM; and Indian Institutes of Technology (IIT), which produce some of the most desired software engineers in the world. It also has more than 250 universities (over 900 colleges) and engineering colleges providing computer education at the degree or diploma level. Their annual output has been constantly increasing since 1985 and reached 130,000 in 2000. The formal education system is complemented by thousands of private training institutes that provide computer education.

In 1998, the Indian government and industry set up the first of several ventures to increase its IT workforce—the Indian Institute of Information Technology (IIIT) at Hyderabad. Besides producing undergraduates and graduates in computer software engineering, IIITs train professionals and industry-sponsored candidates. Private-sector companies, including IBM, Microsoft, Oracle, Satyam, and Metamor, are allowed to affiliate their own schools with the IIITs.

In 2001–2002, NASSCOM conducted a study on human resources in IT. It found that there were 522,000 IT software and services professionals, including professionals engaged in software, IT services, and IT-enabled services. The median age of software professionals was 25.6 years, and 44 percent of them had over three years' working experience. There was an average of six percent rise in basic salary during 2001, with most companies adopting the variable pay concept to link pay to revenues and to control costs.

NASSCOM recommended that to maintain India's competitive advantage of knowledge workers with the right mix of technical, business, and functional skills, the workforce needs to increase by at least 10-fold by 2008 for a total of at least 2.2 million. NASSCOM is pushing the Indian government to undertake several initiatives, including setting up IITs/IIITs in every state and allocating at least 150 billion rupees toward this activity; ensuring that IIT/IIITs offer courses in project management, e-commerce, Java, software engineering, and other skills identified in the NASSCOM study; giving deemed university status for IIITs; encouraging more PhDs to create original technology and to meet the requirements of teaching faculties and industry; training more teachers at all levels; including computer science courses in all engineering programs; providing IT modules to every degree/diploma course; increasing the output of the engineering stream; networking educational institutes; retraining industry experts; and training industry professionals.

Vendors in India have adopted quality standards. By 2002, 42 Indian software companies had the SEI CMM level 5 assessment, and 316 Indian software companies had acquired quality certifications. Indian companies are increasingly adopting the people-capability maturity model (People-CMM), which emphasizes human resources.

According to McKinsey & Company, India has a growing number of vendors successfully working on complex R&D projects across all areas of software and services and performing at the levels of leading global players.

Russia—growing fast in software

Although it has over 10,000 professional programmers, the Russian software market is minuscule compared to that of India. (Russia has no presence in the BPO space.) Market-Visio/EDC recently estimated annual revenue at $150–200 million. The market has been growing by about 50 percent a year, with strong potential for more growth. For this reason, major international companies have established offshore development centers in Russia, including Motorola, Intel, Sun, Boeing, LG, Lucent, and Nortel.

Intel opened a development center in Novgorod in 1993 with 10 programmers, which soon grew to 200, and recently announced plans to expand the number to 500. Motorola, too, started small in 1993. It now has over 200 software engineers in its software manufacturing facilities in St. Petersburg, which has achieved CMM level 5 status. Sun Microsystems, which entered Russia in 1989, is now in partnership with the Moscow Center of SPARC International, employing about 300 programmers, to develop new software and provide support for existing products globally. Russian-owned R&D and software development centers, however, are not on par with Indian centers in their process maturity, having a long way to go to achieve CMM and Six Sigma standards.

Talent access, not cost, must be the primary reason to go to Russia, which offers strong technical capabilities in mathematics and fundamental sciences as well as innovative approaches. It is strongest in R&D, where it has more scientists and engineers working than any other country. Russian labor costs less than that in Western Europe and North America but is about the same as that in India and China.

Russia has about 150 software development vendors, primarily in Moscow, St. Petersburg, and Novosibirsk, whose universities are the top sources of programmers. There are also software development providers in Nizhniy Novgorod, Yekaterinburg, Sarov, and Perm.

The World Bank estimates that Russia has more than one million technically trained personnel, considerably more than the US, China, Japan, and India. Russian programmers have the skills to work on cutting-edge software technology as well as legacy work, made possible by the increasing number of certification centers from Sun, Microsoft, and Novell, as well as small independent schools providing certifications in specific technologies. This means that companies can send high-value development projects to Russia.

According to Microsoft research surveys, within the last seven years, 1.3 million people graduated from Russian universities with the skills to work in the IT industry. But only 70,000 actually work in IT companies in Russia, with 8,000 to 10,000 working in the offshore software industry. Outsourcing-Russia.com, a portal devoted to outsourcing of software development to Russia, estimates that Moscow universities alone graduate about 5,000 to 5,500 IT-related specialists a year and an additional 16,000 to 18,000 programmers in various engineering fields.

Russian labor costs range from $10 to $25 per developer's hour, depending on skills and project size. This rate is slightly lower than India's, where programmers are paid $15 to $30 per hour. Russian companies recently began opening sales and marketing centers in the US and Europe, either directly or through joint ventures.

Sharing European culture and history gives Russia an advantage over other countries in offering offshore services to that continent, as does its physical proximity with most of its software development centers in the European region. IT managers in high-tech companies have the same or higher level of education as their European counterparts. However, English language skills are not as good as Indian programmers, who are educated in English. Also, Russia has few experienced business managers at all levels of business and software development process; however, this is offset by the strong sense of entrepreneurship in its business community.

Russia's economic and political climate has stabilized and improved during Vladimir Putin's presidency, leading to Standard & Poor's and Moody's giving it better debt and credit ratings. Russia plans to initiate legislative, regulatory, and legal reforms to switch to transparent international accounting standards. The government has recognized the importance of the software industry to the country and is introducing tax privileges for software developers and IT specialists. It also plans to introduce incubators to train new entrepreneurs and co-operative research programs, such as the Russian Ministry for Economic Development's $2.6 billion Electronic Russia Program.

China—getting there

China is emerging as a strong contender in offshoring services with its large population of skilled IT labor. Even though it is not yet a mature market in software outsourcing, companies are seriously looking at it, given the success in outsourcing manufacturing activities. China has nearly 200,000 IT professionals in the software export industry, with an additional 50,000 entering the workforce each year. Software engineers and project managers are significantly less expensive than their US counterparts and somewhat less than their Indian ones.

However, there are negative aspects of going to China. Most Chinese IT service employees have strong technical skills but lack proficiency in spoken and written English and knowledge of Western culture, and most project managers are short on experience. Many Chinese prefer to migrate after gaining English language skills and IT experience. The result is very high attrition and instability in the operations. Also, local manufacturing companies absorb a lot of IT talent, leaving little for the offshore needs.

China is an emerging subcontracting center for other offshore vendors, which will enable it to learn global practices before striking out on its own. Chinese IT companies are more comfortable dealing with people of their own culture. In addition, going overseas to grab IT business means facing competition from countries with more experience as well as investing in marketing and sales offices overseas. Hence, the presence of the Chinese on the global IT market is relatively small.

Even though China's infrastructure does not compare with that of the West, it works well for outsourcing software work. China is now investing more in its telecommunications infrastructure and making up for lost time.

The market research firm Gartner estimates that China will emerge as one of the top three countries for overseas IT outsourcing between 2007 and 2010. Although China has not made a dent in the BPO services market in English-speaking Western countries, GE has established BPO centers in China to provide services to Japan. China has more than 40 companies providing outsourced call center services with more than 3,200 seats. Other outsourcing areas include information services (GE electronic data interchange, IBM e-business services), document imaging (Kodak i Center), and logistics (China Logistics).

Despite a worldwide recession, China has the world's second largest economy, primarily due to offshore manufacturing, which reduces the risk of outsourcing there. The Chinese legal system is improving, and several commercial and intellectual property rights laws have recently been passed. But the legal system is not as mature as India's and does not come close to the systems in the US or Europe.

China's entry into the WTO has boosted business confidence in that country. Entering the WTO requires adherence to the rules and practices of the global marketplace. China has made the first step to globalize its economy and benchmark with the leading markets in developed world. China is also a member of the Asia-Pacific Economic Cooperation (APEC). The government has adopted preferential policies, including taxes, industrial parks, and other incentives to attract and develop its high-tech industry. However, China is still closed politically and may conceal fundamental economic weaknesses emerging in the country.

The other disadvantage that China faces is high software piracy. Recently, Cisco ran a sting operation on a leading Chinese company and found that its software code had been copied, including the bugs. A company must seriously consider the piracy problem before exporting IT work to China. Corruption in China is extremely high, which makes dealing with the government officials complex.

The Philippines—emerging BPO player

The Philippines is a former US colony. Its American cultural and communications skills prove appealing to US firms that export processes there even though the cost is slightly higher than in India. In the Philippines, the average salary of an IT employee is $6,564 per year. English fluency makes the Philippines popular as a source of call center operations. Given the compatibility with US, no wonder FedEx, Northwest Airlines, and Walt Disney have set up operations there.

The $1 billion Philippines software industry comprises more than 1,000 companies employing 290,000 professionals in application development, application maintenance, call centers, business continuity and disaster recovery, and e-business. The country has been a strong source of programming skills for more than 20 years, and its IT infrastructure, including telecommunications, originally put in place by the US military, is solid. The Special Economic Zone Act of 1991 established IT parks to support the IT export industry. However, bandwidth can be costly.

The Philippines may not surpass India in software development outsourcing. But in the other outsourcing areas—BPO and contact centers—the Philippines is well established.

The country has a large, skilled labor pool, and universities turn out 350,000 technology-related degrees each year. This output is expected to keep wages from rising too high in the Philippines. The Philippine government is setting up a program to offer incentives for certification. The country is considered a good alternative to India if paying a marginally higher cost is not an issue.

The country, however, suffers from political instability and corruption. Terrorist activities also tarnish the Philippines' image. The Philippines has a short supply of project management talent, but this will be overcome as processes mature. The government provides such incentives as three to six-year income tax breaks and exemptions from all government fees, licenses, dues, and export taxes.

Ireland

Ireland could have been the perfect place to export software and business processes from US and other European countries. The Irish software industry generate revenues of over $6 billion every year. With Irish government incentives to produce software in Ireland, many companies have set up software production for distribution in Europe. Since Ireland is a member in the EU, it gets tax benefits from selling in Europe.

The Irish software industry is very mature and has programmers extremely skilled in the latest technologies. With low turnover, the quality of programmers is excellent. Ireland has moved up the value chain from manufacturing hardware to packaged applications development, concentrating on software license sales. It also has cost-effective and modern telecom architecture. However, cost has driven outsourcing customers away from Ireland to other countries.

The problem with outsourcing to Ireland is the limited number of software programmers it produces. Despite government initiatives, Ireland graduates only 5,000 programmers every year, too low for the country to gain scale of any sort. The short supply of software talent has led to high labor costs. A programmer costs roughly $25,000 to $40,000 per year. Therefore, companies have to look overseas to acquire talent.

Geopolitical stability, process maturity, geographic distance, and culture work well for Ireland, but the country has priced itself out of the offshoring market.

Chapter 8
The Key to Offshoring Success

Once a company has felt the need for offshoring IT or business processes—possibly to access quality talent or to reduce costs—it must follow a plan to fulfill it.

There are four phases to an offshoring processes:
1. Finding a champion to sell the idea of outsourcing

2. Identifying and prioritizing the processes to be outsourced

3. Finding an offshore vendor

4. Executing the contract

The importance of a champion

The one crucial element for success in outsourcing offshore is a champion in top management. Moving processes offshore involves managers going into unknown territory and/or losing power or even losing jobs. No wonder top management is needed to overcome their resistance and bring disparate divisions to accept the vision.

The champion must have a compelling vision to sell internally and convince line managers to buy in. And top management must be committed to it and be prepared for risk and reward. Those who successfully leverage the benefits of offshore outsourcing are rewarded and those who do not are penalized.

Jack Welch had a vision of offshoring and the efficiencies it would bring to GE. His vision was made a reality by Scott Bayman, president and CEO of GE India; Gary Riener, IT leader of GE; Pramod Bhasin, president of GE Capital India; and several other top GE officials. The success of the offshoring initiative was due also to GE's value principles of boundarylessness, stretch, and speed.

When companies grow fast, they tend to build walls, stifle creativity, waste time, and narrow vision, all of which eventually hinder progress. However, through boundarylessness, GE broke down walls and barriers within the company and between GE and other organizations to cultivate the free flow of ideas and improve activities.

Champions of offshore outsourcing have a compelling vision to sell. ABN AMRO's vision was to enhance shareholder value and reduce the total ownership costs of business processes. The Dutch bank found that cutting costs of non-core processes was one route to value. Moving BPO to India was justified by cost alone, as well as the focus on core and talent accesses.

Citibank's Latin American Consumer Bank (LACB) had the vision to improve operational efficiency and reduce costs by consolidating nine technology centers into two in Mexico, which imported talent from India and achieved cost and operational goals. Former Northwestern Mutual CIO, Walt Wojcik, believed that all competitive advantage is temporary, so the IT infrastructure must be in place to take advantage of an opportunity. Since IT was not a core competency, he pushed for offshoring the processes to leverage opportunities in the company's core areas of business. To read more about this company's experiences, see "The Northwestern Mutual Story"

Identifying and prioritizing processes to be outsourced

Having identified a need for outsourcing offshore and found a champion, the company needs to decide which processes to export and then prioritize them. Usually, stable and robust processes with less business dependence are the first to be outsourced since they are not so tightly integrated with other business processes and require less management contact. Most processes outsourced are non-core, including IT functions that actually support core functions. Generally, any process that does not give a competitive edge to a company in the marketplace can be outsourced.

In this process, the entire organization should be mapped to identify high-cost and high-manpower departments. Once the processes are identified, the organization must ascertain if outsourcing them is feasible. For example, certain functions cannot be outsourced for legal reasons and so are off the list.

As the next step, the organization should decide its immediate and medium-term tactical goals, perhaps immediate cost reduction or ease of exporting the process or possibly proven successes in low-risk projects initially. The goals will help determine how the company prioritizes the processes it exports. It can then weight such factors as training and transfer, complexity of skills, risk, cost savings, legal, end-customer preferences and process maturity to make a final decision. End customer preferences are important. For instance the credit card holders of a bank may not prefer talking to an offshore vendor's employees. Several processes have been recalled from offshore locations after end customer objections.

The amount of time training and transfer of processes take depends not only on their complexity but also, more importantly, on the availability of trainers. Without trainers, it's best to move the process later. This factor usually gets a high weight in prioritizing. Complexity of the process can be ameliorated with the right trainers. If the risk of transferring the process is high due to complexity and lack of trainers, it makes no sense to move the process out early, even if the cost savings are high.

The maturity of the process is also important. In GE, the vendor's process maturity levels determine whether to "ship and fix" or "fix and ship" a broken process. The former is preferable for high levels; the latter for low. Also if the relationship with the vendor is long, clients are comfortable to ship and fix the process.

Before seeking an offshore vendor, a company can prepare for the offshoring exercise. First, it should set up a team with top management to plan, monitor, and oversee the search and transition to outsourcing. This team will include people from the information systems division, key user groups, and executive management, including marketing and/or strategy management.

The company must allocate internal resources to help manage its relationship with the offshore outsourcer. Before exporting them, it should measure current software systems and business processes to benchmark them in terms of service capability, performance, uptime, costs, user satisfaction, and other parameters relevant to the company.

Once the company has outsourced processes, its strategic direction changes, with the re-allocation or dismissal of resources and the focus on core. Therefore, it must rework its strategic business plan before outsourcing. Since an outsourcing agreement typically covers a period of seven to ten years (or even longer), the company will need to chart a path for that time frame. With the decoupling of the non-core functions, it will need to know where it is going locally and globally in terms of products, markets, manufacturing, sources of supply, distribution arrangements, and labor sources.

If it is outsourcing IT processes, the company must have a 10-year systems plan. This will identify long-term needs in the area of new applications, those to be updated or discontinued, and those to be modified. If it is outsourcing business processes, the company must have a plan, which sets out what it will try to achieve in its core area of business and which contextual resources are needed to support the initiative.

The company should have several process alternatives, which the chosen vendor can run before making the final choice: software and hardware in IT or communication infrastructure and the ways to run the processes remotely in BPO.

Most important, the company must know its cost structure and use it as a base to estimate future costs to create and support the offshore initiative. Looking at the next five to ten years, it must: estimate all relevant capital and operating costs; interest costs; residual value of equipment and facilities; cost of transition, including personnel; cost of changes in direction and level of resources; and cost of contract modification. Management may want to seek expert advice from external consultants.

The company should review the strengths and weaknesses of the offshoring alternative to determine if it will help its long-term goals. After all, going offshore must be better than staying on-site.

To guide the company through the outsourcing decision, selection, and contracting processes, management can set up an expert team with internal and external experts in outsourcing, information technology, business processes, and legal matters. This team administers the contract over time, assures a smooth migration to the new systems, and resolves problems that will arise after the contract is signed.

Finding an offshore vendor

To find an offshore vendor, a company can use a consultant or do the search itself. A consultant will guide the company through supplier selection, due diligence, negotiation, and contracting—a good route to take for a company with no experience in offshore outsourcing. A consultant also provides information on offshore markets, processes, and players, and helps create an offshore strategy. Even after the process has been outsourced, it can help improve performance throughout the project life cycle.

A company seeking an offshore vendor on its own must: prepare a bid package with objectives, specifications, time frame and quality expectations, and criteria; identify potential vendors; request proposals and detailed vendor information; and award the project to a vendor.

Identifying a country to outsource to

In moving IT and business processes offshore, selecting a vendor is often based on the country the company wants to outsource to—India, China, the Philippines, Russia, or Ireland, based on geopolitical risks, knowledge-domain strengths, talent pool, comparative costs, and work culture. For the first item, it can find reports from such credit rating agencies as Moody's and Standard & Poor's. For information on countries, see Chapter 7.

Preparing a bid proposal

Once the company has identified several likely outsourcing suppliers, it sends them a request for information (RFI), which outlines the services it needs. The RFI should provide enough information to potential suppliers to determine if they have the interest and skills needed to do the job requested.

The RFI process must have deadlines for publishing the request for qualifications, receiving qualifications, and shortlisting and notifying bidders.

From the responses to its RFI, the company can create a shortlist of offshoring vendors (no more than six) it feels comfortable with and would like to consider.

Chapter 8

Sending out a request for proposal

The next step is to create a request for proposal (RFP) to send to those vendors identified as able to deliver the required service. (If a company is entering the offshore space for the first time, it is best to invite several vendors to respond to the RFP.) This document will identify the elements that mean success and failure to the company, such as quality, delivery dates, acceptance criteria, and problem resolution. It will define exactly what the company needs and/or what it wants the product or service to accomplish—what it wants out of its relationship with the vendor. If management is unable to write down its needs, a consultant can help the company through the process.

The biggest challenge in developing the RFP is to write all the details of an offshore project or service. But this is the best way to attract well-considered and reasonable proposals from vendors, which will establish a comfortable working relationship through complicated offshore services.

To facilitate objective comparisons of proposals from different vendors, the organization should create a template for vendor responses in a tight format, requesting specific facts and figures. The RFP should request this information: a description of the vendor's project development approach and costs; their corporate information, including financial details; qualifications, including previous clients with contact information and relevant URLs; a description of their development process; details of the service delivery methods; project stages; milestones; quality control; testing; proposed team and their qualifications; proposed schedule; costs and payment details; and terms and conditions.

To be fair to both company and vendors, the RFP process must have deadlines for responding to the RFP, informing the successful bidder, signing the purchase order, conducting a scoping meeting, commencing project development or service delivery, and signing off on project delivery or a milestone that states that a process is running as specified. The RFP should go out eight to ten weeks before requested submission date: Considering and writing a detailed proposal takes time.

The company should give the vendors a single contact person, who can answer questions about the proposal or the work involved. (Depending on the project, there may be one contact person for contractual matters and one for technical matters.)

It is important to say that the RFP is a private document and cannot be shown to others without the company's permission. Offshore vendors should tell the company upfront if they use freelancers and part-time help. Because of the increased risk of the RFP getting into the hands of competition, the organization should insist on any freelance proposal writers signing a non-disclosure agreement.

The RFP should be divided into three sections: overview, technical, and time-cost. The overview section requests such information about the vendor company as its vision and financials. The technical section includes time frames, projected required personnel, and schedules for completing the project. The time-cost section enables the vendor to detail the time and costs that will be required to complete the project. The vendor can also provide a short product demo and references from former clients.

The RFP should include:

- An executive summary, which describes the organization's business, market position, and revenue, and outlines the business and technical reasons for considering offshore outsourcing.

- A schedule of events with a timeline for the vendors, including the date of the RFP release, proposal deadline, vendor presentations, contract award, and letter of intent, as well as evaluation procedures and criteria.

- A definition of the expected proposal format, to whom and how the proposal should be delivered (including number of copies) and how questions regarding the RFP will be handled (e.g., Will all vendors' questions and answers to all parties involved be published?).

- Letter of transmittal, which defines the content of each responding vendor's cover letter. The company should require an officer of the vendor to sign the letter to ensure the vendor's bid has management approval and backing.

- The section layout of all vendor proposals. Ensuring consistent proposal format and content will save time in evaluating and comparing proposals.

- Pointed questions to gain a comprehensive understanding of each vendor's service offering, including an in-house domain expert if necessary.

- An overview of the company's environment, including the number of telecommuters, geographic dispersion, applications, equipment, software, security, network infrastructure, network management, helpdesk, and network service levels.

- Equipment/FTE (full-time equivalent) specifications. This must clearly state equipment needs and the number of FTEs whose jobs will be transferred in case of BPO. It provides the specifications of the software that the vendor must supply or manage.

- The company's expectations for installation, project management, maintenance, and service delivery to discover if the vendor's personnel are qualified and able to deliver the service.

- The organization's performance management and reporting needs.

- Outline of faults for which the vendor shall assume responsibility. Without defining boundaries of responsibility, problems can arise in the relationship for the life of the contract.

- Security management—how the vendor will protect the company's business from intrusion and secure its network and process.

- Asset management—Because outsourcing implies giving up control of one's network, the vendor must have a plan for managing and tracking its assets. Poor asset management can lead to extended outages.

The RFP process has limitations. In the end, the relationship between company and vendor is based on trust. During the software development or service delivery process, there will be errors on both sides and delays in deliveries due to geographic distances, and the relationship must be built to survive these hurdles. A proposal can tell a limited amount about a company and nothing about the intangibles.

Evaluating the vendors

As the vendors are working on their proposals, the company should develop a method of evaluating them, determining the criteria and deciding the order of their importance. Spreadsheets with both qualitative and quantitative assessments can help make side-by-side comparisons of all the proposals.

In broad terms, the key factors to evaluating a vendor include management experience; international experience; employee retention; technology, power, and telecom facilities and back-up; cost; transparency in billing structure; disaster recovery and business continuity plan; soft skills like language and cultural adaptability; financial viability; and technology expertise.

To help determine an overall feel for vendors' responses, the qualitative assessment should include these variables:

- Understanding business requirements: The vendor must know the company's industry to enable it to understand the business needs and so create optimum software or BPO solutions.

- Flexibility: It is best not to do business with a vendor with rigid processes and unwillingness to change to accommodate the company's needs.

- Feedback from former and existing clients: Feedback from both satisfied and unsatisfied customers reveals the strengths and weaknesses of the vendor.

- Employees' communication skills: Communication gaps can lead to project mishaps in day-to-day operations. In the call center space, ask for recorded calls of the vendor.

- Commitment to win the bid: Overcommitting shows desperation on the part of a vendor to win a bid and leads to unrealized expectations later in the relationship with the company.

- Quality of technical personnel and management: This is crucial to the success of any offshore initiative.

- Management structure: The closer the account manager to the top, the better attention the account will get.

- Management bandwidth: The customer list will indicate the size of the vendor's existing contracts. A small account may get very little management attention from any but a small vendor.

- Credit reports: Reports by such organizations as Dun & Bradstreet will indicate the solvency of the vendor.

- Process and tools: The vendor's business should be process driven, not personality driven. A process-driven company will continue to give consistent service even when people running the process leave. Most professional companies use online project management tools to monitor processes.

- IP protection: The company should audit the measures the vendor uses to protect IP and its enforcement.

- Relationship management: A vendor with a lot of repeat business has good customer relationship management.

- Quality certifications: Independent quality certification is good guide to the vendor's process maturity. However, most certifications apply to a specific division and not the whole company.

The quantitative assessment is based on replies to the questions asked in the RFP, weighted by the company's criteria:

- Telecom infrastructure: This is crucial for communications and delivery of services.

- Fixed infrastructure: Ownership or lease of land and buildings indicates the stability of the vendor.

- Geographic presence: A wider geographic presence indicates greater market penetration and a diversified client portfolio that mitigates risk. It's also good from a disaster- recovery and business-continuity point of view.

- Cost: Although inexpensive is good, "very cheap" may mean that the vendor needs closer scrutiny. Vendors' fixed and variable costs will show if they will make money from the contract or if they are desperate to get business.

- Physical proximity: Having a vendor representative with on-site presence near the customer's location can solve many operational hurdles.

- Financial stability: Financial statements should ensure business continuity. Outsourcing information and business processing needs, ranging from some resources to the entire information technology or HR function, puts mission-critical activity in the hands of vendor. No company wants a vendor going out of business after it has exported critical functions.

- Ramp-up capability: A vendor's history will show how quickly it can ramp up to meet rapidly changing requirements. A slow vendor can lengthen time-to-market on new products.

- Operating and transfer cost: Based on their revenues, the vendor should be able to sustain these costs.

- Size of the skill base: A wide skill base cushions attrition better. Also the vendor can pull resources from within the company to meet surging needs of the customer and not look outside. Hiring resources takes longer than re-allocating resources internally.

- Shadow resource policy: Vendors that supplement their core team with additional non-billable resources as "shadow resources" provides risk mitigation with attrition as well as help in quick ramping up.

- Offshore outsourcing experience: Getting a vendor with maximum experience is a good risk-mitigating strategy. An organization needs to know how long the offshore service provider has been in the business and how much of its revenue comes from offshore outsourcing and how much from providing services on-site. The best vendor is one whose offshore revenues are more than its on-site revenues.

- Appropriate size: Large vendors will usually not pay attention to small accounts.

- Thought leadership: Vendors that have excelled in a specific industry or technology or practice domain often are good bets. They often present their approaches to solving complex problems in seminars and symposiums and publish white papers on their Web sites and occasionally in refereed journals.

- Standard practices: Flexible and proven practices will give the offshore vendor the base and the tools to create an environment to meet a company's specific needs. Standard practices should be fully documented and have worked successfully in the past. If there have been failures, the vendor should explain them.

A company has to look beyond the vendor's proposal in evaluating it. It should check the reputation of the vendor with its employees and bankers, and with other vendors to find out about top management, project management, programming, and testing talent, which are key to delivering services. Since the way a vendor treats its employees reflects its ability to hire expertise crucial for the success of a project, it is best to avoid companies with high attrition rates. The vendor also needs adequate staff in consulting, analysis, design, programming, and testing. When possible, the company should check how the vendor runs the offshore centers by visiting them and auditing the training provided to it's staff.

An organization needs to confirm that the vendor has the expertise in its industry and can predict current and future industry needs. This is critical in regulated industries or those undergoing legislative changes, such as health care and insurance. In the BPO space, especially, industry vertical domain knowledge is extremely important. Once the process is outsourced, the company will fast lose knowledge of it and will have to rely on the outsourcer.

Since offshore outsourcing is about taking processes out of the country, a company should look for one outsourcer to handle current and future needs. Having multiple vendors or changing vendors can result in increased knowledge transfer costs. This is particularly necessary for testing interfaces on different platforms, in different languages, and between different systems worldwide.

To ensure a vendor's financial strength, the company should perform due diligence—a thorough examination of financial statements, press reports, Internet information, corporate organization and strategic plans, and corporate culture and history.

Looking at repeat customers will indicate customer satisfaction. Good current customer references are perhaps the most important criteria in judging outsourcers. While nobody likes to admit they selected the wrong outsourcing partner, they will say if they have expanded their relationship with the vendor; if they haven't, there may be a problem with the vendor. One can also ask these customers how the offshoring initiative would be run differently if done again to gain clues to the relationship with the existing vendor. Examining the vendor's criteria for selecting new customers and its history of any litigation, including wins and losses and settlements, will tell what mistakes the outsourcer has made and whether it has learned any lessons.

Successful outsourcers have most likely engaged in strategic alliances and relationships with other parties, such as tool-set providers, methodology companies/consultants, testing houses, disaster recovery companies, and special leading edge integrators. Since these provide ready access to resources and tools that may otherwise be scarce, a company should examine how these relationships and/or tools have been integrated and used by the outsourcer before and to what extent they might be needed and integrated into its own needs.

Once proposals start coming in, the company's outsourcing team should read them several times and complete the evaluation forms, considering only the proposals that address everything they are looking for and discarding the incomplete ones. They should analyze the technical and operational aspects first, ranking them on established metrics, to avoid being biased by costs; if the vendor is low cost, they may be tempted to ease the evaluation criteria on the other parameters.

Several companies give a high weight to technology—about 60 percent. This criterion takes into account such factors as the educational level of the vendor's personnel, the experience of the vendor, and the vendor's management in your industry. A North American telecom company planning to outsource $10 million worth of work offshore selected five finalists from the RFP processes and asked every vendor what it should be concerned about in respect to the others. This strategy gave the telecom company a lot of insight into the weaknesses of all the vendors.

Technological, or domain, expertise and stability of the vendor are important. If everything else is equal, a company should opt for the larger player for stability. If stability and technical expertise are the same, it can opt for a vendor based on price, which should not get a weight of more than 40 percent.

After the technical evaluation, the company should analyze the overall financial condition of the vendor, including its financial standing, capacity capability, management capability, and service capability. After grading all proposals, the team should review each one to see if the grades need to change.

Selecting the vendor

Once the team has shortlisted the vendors based on their proposals, they should set up short meetings with them for a final qualitative assessment. The meeting can be a forum to discuss what the company envisions in outsourcing, as well as to garner ideas, suggestions, and possible solutions for its problem. Most vendors are willing to take a couple of hours to help. The team should be informal, open, honest, and should promise nothing.

Having evaluated the vendors based on their proposals and presentations, the team should consider the best. If they like more than one vendor to outsource to, they should go for the "best and final offer." The company can also pit one vendor against the other to get the best offer, which can get much better offers on price, flexibility, and project completion time.

Sometimes, two vendors work on a project—a primary vendor doing a major chunk of the job and a secondary vendor. This strategy means that the company does not totally rely on one vendor; the next vendor can take over if the first vendor fails, without disrupting the project. Several companies like GE and Eastman Kodak have multiple vendors. The downside of this strategy is that time must be devoted to vendor management. It is a good strategy to adopt for big-budget offshoring, but for smaller projects, selecting a single vendor is better.

Once the company has notified the vendor that has won the project, it should inform the other vendors why they lost, which will help them in future.

The company should ensure that it awards the contract on the date indicated in the RFP, since vendors often must schedule staff and resources to complete projects. Being indecisive about awarding or starting a project sends a message to the vendor that not adhering to timelines is acceptable. This will hurt the relationship.

The contract between company and vendor must enable a fair relationship and have clauses and incentives to make both parties perform. If the outsourcer presents a contract that is too good to be true, it may be just trying to win the contract; if it has such contracts with other customers, it will doubtlessly have problems fulfilling its obligations, leading to litigation.

The process of negotiating the contract and reaching a consensus on difficult alternatives is a preview of how the future relationship will work. It is best to abandon a vendor that is too rigid. How the outsourcer handles negotiating the contract and how willing it is to listen to a company's needs and modify its approach will indicate whether the offshore outsourcing relationship will be successful.

Executing the contract

Once the company and vendor have signed the deal, project execution starts, often with the signing of service level agreements (SLAs). These informal contracts establish objective performance criteria. They assign responsibilities to employees of both organizations, quantifying performance parameters to improve the outsourcing process. SLAs also fix accountability and responsibility for day-to-day operations and define the penalty if the vendor does not meet its terms. SLAs have a service definition, performance tracking, problem management, fees and expenses, customer duties, warranties and remedies, security, legal compliance, and termination. Generally, SLAs complement other contractual agreements that cover a variety of details, including corrective actions, penalties and incentives, dispute-resolution procedures, nonconformance, acceptable service violations, reporting policies, and rules for terminating a contract.

A SLA should detail the responsibilities of the offshore vendor, the rights of the customer, and the penalties assessed when the service provider violates any element of it. It also identifies and defines the service offering itself, plus the supported products, evaluation criteria, and quality of service that customers should expect.

SLAs for different industries contain different sets of metrics, elements, tolerance ranges, and criteria for calculating these. For instance, the network SLA would include details on bandwidth, performance, and service quality. SLAs should also detail the nature and types of tools required for users and service providers to monitor and manage them.

Effective SLAs levy penalties against service providers that violate the terms of their contracts. Generally, these come as credits against future service. In addition to refunds for lost time or poor performance, penalties for SLA violations should also consider the impact of a violation on an enterprise's business.

SLAs are key in outsourcing projects to guarantee superior service levels. Mission-critical applications must be available and responsive; software quality must improve; support calls should be resolved quickly before they affect productivity. SLAs take these into account and put in place processes to measure, report, and analyze vendor performance and pinpoint areas for improvement.

The research firm IDC notes that nearly 97 percent of the large companies (2,500 or more employees) it queried required a SLA for network availability in the next 12 months. SLAs are the key to ensuring consistent quality and uptime in business-critical computing environments. The same holds true of BPO services. Several companies provide managing and service contract capabilities and tools to build and track SLAs, such as Firehunter from Agilent Technologies and Eccord Enterprise from Eccord Systems.

The company and supplier must establish project estimation and milestone methods. Having a good idea of how long it would take to complete a project allows the company to guide its vendor to do it. A set of tangible milestones that can be validated will allow the teams to stay on track or make corrections in a timely manner.

To ensure success of the project or service, the company needs to put together an empowered management team to execute the offshoring exercise. The team leader, ideally a top manager with the authority to drive processes, needs to be involved only in the early stages. Once the organization has accepted that offshore outsourcing is a way of doing business, other managers can take over its leadership. The organization should put in place a decision-making structure. Communication and execution of decisions should be seamless between the company and its service provider.

Both organizations should agree on and implement a management reporting process to ensure a harmonious relationship. The outsourcing contract should dictate specific goals and expectations along with the costs and project milestones that need to be reported.

The offshoring teams of both organizations should leverage in-house expertise and knowledge. During the initial stages of the project, the in-house experts guide the service provider in the processes that need to be sent offshore. Once the process is sent offshore and its quality improved, the supplier's newly learnt expertise should help the company's in-house staff do their jobs better.

The process will transfer knowledge from internal staff to vendor teams, resulting in its codification, documentation, and publication electronically or physically to make knowledge a common resource. This is critical to the success of the project.

By treating its supplier as a partner, the company can think about strategic improvement. Outsourcing can bring immediate benefits in terms of costs. But a company can experience long-term benefits from the offshore initiative by allowing the service provider to expand the initial service. Allowing the vendor to re-engineer the company's processes gives the greatest benefits over time in terms of cost and customer satisfaction.

To make offshore outsourcing a way of life in an organization, a senior manager should be the chief resource officer (CRO), acting as a liaison between the company and the outsourcing provider. This will signal the importance of offshore outsourcing to the organization and quickly make it acceptable with line managers.

The CRO should schedule formal meetings with the vendor at regular intervals to get reports on the current status of service and to establish whether the offshore vendor has met performance levels based on previously set standards. Corrective action should be taken if performance does not meet the standards. The process should also be reviewed for possible improvements.

To measure improvements, processes should be baselined and benchmarked. The baseline is where the process is in the beginning; a benchmark is usually the global standard, which should be achieved or surpassed. With a call center, for example, a company needs to know how well it is performing on call outcome and call production. By evaluating and justifying marketing campaign costs through comparative studies, a benchmarking process can determine if a call center meets best-in-class or even world-class benchmark standards. Productivity and customer service benchmarking allows management to keep the vendor call center on track and running the right campaigns.

Benchmarking enables a company to generate real-time reports and rate the ability of a call center to meet its needs, spot any performance gaps or service levels that need attending to, and demonstrate first-hand the benefits in outsourcing that can be used to sell the process within the organization. Benchmarking and quality targets to be achieved should be part of a SLA.

Transitioning processes

This stage can make or break the exporting of a process. After the contract is signed, the company's outsourcing team has to inform employees that their jobs are being moved offshore. The team must handle this process carefully, especially as some soon-redundant employees will be needed to help in the training and knowledge transfer part of the process; if they walk out, the offshoring process will be stalled. The company must be prepared to offer these employees incentives—in the form of cash or assurance of redeployment—to stay on until the process is offshored.

The transition process can be executed either on-site or remotely. In an on-site scenario, some of the vendor's employees fly to the client's location for training for an extended period and then train their colleagues at the remote site. A relatively inexpensive transitioning is through teleconferencing or flying the trainer offshore to conduct the training.

Supervising offshored processes

The company must decide how it will govern the offshore initiative. In a centralized model, all the governance and supervision authority falls on a central authority, which is cost-effective and easy to manage. However, this keeps the users of the service at a distance from the supervisory process, so the two may be out of sync. To prevent this, resources from line functions that work directly with the vendor can support the authority. However, this needs additional staffing and requires effective co-ordination between the line resources and the central authority, thus increasing costs.

Another model has the central authority primarily responsible for governance but individual departments using the services of the offshore provider to ensure compliance. These report to both the line manager and the central supervisory authority. This needs greater co-ordinating among many more players and faces the problem of dual reporting relationships and the high administrative and staff costs of supporting multiple IT and BPO users.

In the decentralized model, governance resources report to the line manager. This approach gives line managers the control on governance and closely aligns governance to the offshore service delivery needs. The cost of the decentralized approach is high and does not leverage enterprise knowledge, information, or processing. Duplicate governance efforts are likely and costly.

Meeting the challenges

Several challenges can threaten the success of offshore outsourcing relationships.

The company can lose management control over the project or service if the exported processes are not stable or fixed before shipping. To prevent this, the company should structure its SLAs and use tools that give visibility into the software development or business process offshore, and hold regular meetings with the vendor's team to see how the process is being executed and if corrective action is needed.

Integrating the offshored process with the business can be extremely difficult. However, ensuring that the business rules and process interfaces are well defined, documented, and understood will help. The company also needs a direct reporting line between the vendor's line manager and its own, with dotted lines to the top management of both entities. In GE's R&D center in India, the head of the GE Plastics division in India reports directly to GE Plastics in the US. But he also has a dotted reporting line to the head of the R&D center in India.

Outsourcing can easily fail if the business does not a set of repeatable internal processes to ensure that it can provide clear directions, specifications, objectives, time frames, quality, and communications with outsourcing vendors. This can result in missed deadlines, poor product quality, and future internal resistance to using offshore resources. A poorly executed outsourcing project will create a negative reputation for the company's manager and the vendor.

A company should ensure that it delivers accurate, clear, and concise specifications. Extending these processes to the offshore vendor enables seamless specification writing and understanding, with little or no questions and clarifications going back and forth.

The build-and-release management of the project is another challenge. With an IT project, the company must assess its basic software development infrastructure, including configuration management, defect tracking and management, and release control, so it can share its environment with the offshore vendor and map it to the remote location. Offshore vendors can provide the expertise in this area. The vendor must also agree to and meet the company's quality goals for function, usability, reliability, performance, supportability, scalability, installation, maintenance, and upgrades.

Cross-border communication can create service delivery issues. A company must determine how well its team will work with an offshore team from a totally different culture. Only through effective communication can the task get done and collaboration be successful. Both sets of employees should undergo a sensitivity training program that highlights such matters as the difference in the ways of working in different countries, tolerance for an accent, and accommodating time zone differences for conference calls. As they work together, they will realize other areas that need understanding.

When moving a function to a different country, a company must look at the geopolitical stability of the nation. Since an emergency can lead to long down times and sometimes total disruption of service, the company should put in place a strong disaster recovery and business continuity plan to mitigate the risk.

Chapter 9
Offshoring and Shifting Jobs

Offshore outsourcing's economic and political impact creates both strong proponents for the initiative and vociferous opponents. It affects the balance of trade, spurs political debate and legislation, creates media controversy. Many see offshore outsourcing as a zero sum game, as it shifts jobs and value addition from one location to the other. This is true in the short run, but over the long term, the initiative benefits economies, companies, and labor.

However, in the short to medium term, the upheaval creates a lot of pain. Long-term economic benefits do not ease the immediate hardships of job loss. Though benefits of offshore outsourcing eventually trickle down in terms of inexpensive goods and services and greater global trade, it does not sell with people who cannot put dinner on the table. What is the reason for this turmoil in the US market? What is the future of offshore outsourcing, and how will it affect the social, economic, and political scenario in the developed economies?

Job shift and emerging scenarios

Corporations often need to go offshore because labor laws in developed countries place physical and monetary restrictions on the free flow of labor resources. Qualified professionals cannot freely enter the US, for example, and take up jobs. They have to go through a visa process, and the employers have to pay stipulated minimum wages. The laws are designed to protect the American worker, but the complex process and quantity limitations have driven employers to shift jobs overseas rather than bring employees on-site.

Under the American H1B visa requirement, workers can be hired in "specialty occupations." However, the employer must demonstrate that the person hired has the minimum capability to perform the job and that a person with similar skills is not available in the US. The foreign national must also have the required degree or its equivalent in a subject closely related to the position. Another requirement is that if the employer's business restricts providing employment to the H1B worker, the employer still has to pay the full salary, a rule that does not apply to local labor.

115

The employer has to file a labor condition application (LCA) with the US Department of Labor in the region where the foreign national will work and must prove the foreign employee will receive the prevailing wage (by state-accepted published survey) or higher, at least $60,000. The employer needs to give notice of the LCA to the relevant collective bargaining unit if the job is unionized. If not, it has to be posted in a location so that other employees can see it and apply if needed.

Once the labor department accepts the application, the employer has to apply to the Immigration and Naturalization Service (INS) for the H1B visa, detailing the operations and viability of the company, the job opening, and the prospective employee's background and degree. Even when the INS accepts the H1B application, the maximum stay is usually six years. If an employer has filed for permanent residency of the worker, the employee may be able to stay as long as the worker wishes. With a six-year limit, the employer cannot take a long-term view of the employee and so may find it difficult to execute long-term business plans. Medical research projects stretch over several years, for example, and immigration uncertainty is the last thing an employer needs. A limited number of H1B visas are issued each year: 195,000 for fiscal years 2001 through 2003, and 65,000 a year thereafter.

Professionals can also work in the US on an L visa. This category is for an intra-company transferee where an employee of a company abroad can be brought to its US affiliate, parent, or subsidiary entity on a temporary work basis. The employee must have worked for the company abroad for at least six months and should continue working for the same employer.

There is no minimum wage requirement for the L1 category. The employer has only to prove the existence of the two business entities—one in the US and the other abroad—and establish the requisite relationship. Jobs on an L visa can be offered only for a position of higher-level manager, executive, or "person with specialized knowledge."

Several software services companies have been bringing foreign workers into the US under the L1 category with its easier rules. However, once the employees are in the US, the companies place them to work at the customer's site, which is essentially a different company. This violates the spirit of the law, and the INS has been moving to curb the practice. It may change the law requiring that employees placed at the customer site should be under the H1B category. However, the tightening of the L visa requirement will only lead to more jobs going offshore.

Companies move processes partly to cut costs but also to gain the benefits of scale, quality, speed, and focus on core competence. Outsourcing the process to a vendor in the country also delivers these benefits, but the cost is still high due to more expensive labor and infrastructure.

Minimum wage and visa regulations prevents lowering labor costs in developed countries. In exporting jobs, the value added in a production or service cycle is moved out of the country, as is the wealth that the value-adding process generates. However, a foreign worker retaining a job in the country still pays taxes and spends money there.

Therefore, it is better to retain the job within the country, which can happen only if the wage and visa regulations are relaxed and global supply and demand for talent determine the cost and flow of labor. It is the demand for goods and services that determines their price and the markets in which they will be sold. While regulations in the US ensuring free competition determine the price of several goods and services on a global scale, this is not true of labor. If the US government wants to prevent the medium-term pain to local labor from export of processes, it must either allow inexpensive labor to enter the country, just as it allows goods and services to, or pass regulations preventing the export of jobs. Allowing free flow of labor is politically difficult, and preventing export of jobs will be strongly opposed by businesses.

Future political and trade scenario

The issue of job losses is expected to become a major concern in politics. No politicians like their voters to lose jobs, a prospect that has spurred US politicians to propose legislation to prevent offshore outsourcing.

Trade wars are also in the offing. People against offshore outsourcing will ask that duties be levied on exported services. There could also be issues of quotas like those applied on textiles imported into the US. National governments could fight over subsidies in education and allowing freer trade. The political and trade landscape is going to see several changes due to offshore outsourcing.

117

Chapter 10
Political Relations and Changing Economies

Forrester Research predicts that more that 3.3 million white-collar service jobs and $136 billion in wages will be moved overseas over the next 15 years. These potential job losses are prompting union protests and congressional hearings. States are introducing legislation to keep jobs in the US by blocking companies from using foreign workers on state contracts. A recent study by the Outsourcing Institute found that 60 percent of companies with fewer than 500 employees expect to spend up to $5 million on outsourcing in the next 12 months for technology, manufacturing, and logistics. This means that the largest provider of jobs—small and medium companies—will also send jobs offshore, drastically affecting the employment market in the US.

Legislative issues

The first reactive step is the introduction of legislation by the states to prevent offshoring state contracts, such as the New Jersey bill discussed in Chapter 2. However, the federal government, which controls foreign policy, will strike down any state bills to prevent trade. For example, the US Supreme Court struck down a 1996 Massachusetts procurement law providing sanctions aimed at alleged human rights abuses in Myanmar. The National Foreign Trade Council (NFTC), which examines state sanctions to ensure they do not damage American competitiveness, brought the lawsuit against the state. Even the Clinton administration argued that Massachusetts unlawfully meddled in US foreign policy by limiting state purchases from companies that do business in Myanmar.

Some justices appeared to agree. Justice Ruth Bader Ginsburg asked: "For Massachusetts to go it on its own when the United States is saying we want to get together with our world neighbors... isn't there a clash?" Justice Stephen G. Breyer wondered if states also could enact purchasing policies intended to influence the actions of other states, resulting in "a kind of nightmare" or "chaos." The Massachusetts law said that most companies doing business with Myanmar can sell goods and services to the state only if their bid is 10 percent lower than all other bids. After the trade council challenged the law in 1998, the Court of Appeals ruled it interfered with federal foreign policy and was pre-empted by the federal government's own sanctions. The court went on to state that "the President's maximum power to persuade rests on his capacity to bargain for the benefits of access to the entire national economy without exception for enclaves fenced off willy-nilly by inconsistent political tactics."

If the Massachusetts law had been upheld or several states passed laws similar to the New Jersey outsourcing bill, US businesses would face an increasing number of different and potentially conflicting state and local sanctions laws. This would disrupt and fragment US domestic and foreign commerce.

Any state offshoring bill prevents the federal government from speaking with one voice on foreign commerce. Such bills can carve up the US and international markets. It could result in 50 state bills on offshore outsourcing—a huge problem for a company with offices all over the US. Each additional state and local sanctions law also increases the risk of foreign retaliation against the US as a whole. While the state governments' ability to restrict offshore outsourcing is limited, the federal government's is not. However, it is unlikely that the federal government will prevent offshore outsourcing, as it eventually affects global trade and politics.

Other governments are trying to create hurdles in offshore outsourcing. In the UK, perturbed over continuing job losses, chairman of the House of Commons Trade and Industry Select Committee, Martin O'Neill, stated: "We will be raising the issue of the removal of UK jobs to call centres in places like India." O'Neill will quiz British Telecom over the loss of call center jobs at a hearing that will be part of a wider inquiry into the failure of the IT revolution to deliver the expected jobs miracle, a report in *The Independent* said.

By the end of 2003, HSBC plans to employ 8,000 people in India, China, and Malaysia; British Telecom is planning to create 2,200 new call center posts in India; and Aviva, the insurance company, plans a 1,000-person call center and claims-processing unit in India.

In the US, legislation is pending in Congress to amend visa regulations to prevent employees of offshore vendors on L1 visas from working on customer sites and to scrap H1B visas. If passed, both bills will push customers to send processes offshore, as it will be difficult or impossible to get offshore talent to work on-site.

Erosion of offshoring competitiveness

The cost and quality competitiveness of offshore vendors is expected to come under strain over the next five to seven years. The demand for offshoring has soared, especially in the business process space. Multinational companies have aggressively entered India and hired talent to ramp up operations. As multinational companies poach from Indian companies by offering 40 to 60 percent higher salaries, the offshore wage structure is undergoing a drastic change.

Indian offshore vendors are forced to offer higher salaries to retain people and to hire fresh talent from graduate schools. The rise in wages is expected to slowly eat into the cost-competitiveness of offshore vendors. If the cost differential is not substantial, it will no longer make sense to export processes offshore. For instance, in the call center space, the cost benefit is about 30 percent. If it falls to, say, 15 percent, it will not be worth transferring call centers overseas, especially small call centers currently onshore. And call centers overseas will have to improve the cost benefit by better use of overhead.

As offshoring operations expand, it will be difficult for vendors to maintain quality. The rapid growth has already resulted in a shortage of middle-level managers; consequently, people without requisite experience have been promoted, which will have a negative effect on quality, a core competency of the offshore vendor. A fall in quality may result in high-value processes being retained on-site.

As the currency of India and other developing countries appreciates against the dollar, offshoring will lose its cost advantage. To remain competitive in the long term, it is imperative that offshore vendors and the countries work to retain and improve the cost and quality advantage.

Global trade and political relations

Offshore outsourcing touches different cultures, people, countries, governments, and companies. It consequently affects global trade and political relations between the countries involved. It pushes governments to take action to either further trade or erect trade barriers to better the lives of their populace. Offshore outsourcing is just beginning to hit the newspaper headlines, and governments are going to act.

Most calls for sanctions are issued when there is talk of poor treatment of labor in foreign countries. In China, there was a controversy about using prison labor. In India, sweatshop issues come up, but these will unlikely have a big impact. The work environment and culture in India are world class, but the work schedule is strenuous. Especially in the call center arena, employees are exposed to a host of health problems, as they are up all night answering calls. But these will not be reason enough to create trade barriers

Trade barriers could be erected on the basis of education subsidies. In the US, college eduction has to be paid for privately and is expensive, especially in highly specialized fields like software engineering. On the other hand, education at all levels in India is subsidized by the government. This makes it harder for an American to earn a software engineering degree in comparison to an Indian student. And when Indian graduates enter the workforce, they do not have student loans to pay off; therefore, they are available at a much lower price than the indebted US graduate. As the WTO moves to eliminate subsidies, this will turn out to be an issue of contention.

There could be a pressure on India to stop education subsidies or face penal tariffs. The former might not be possible, and service imports to the developed world may face duties, pushing up the cost. This may take away the financial advantage of sending processes offshore, depending on the level of tariffs.

Labor unions are asking the US government to levy taxes on services. This undesirable action would hurt both the offshore companies and their customers in the US. It is also extremely difficult to keep track of services imported into a country, as no physical goods pass through the customs. Most of the levies will have to be based on invoices, and there will be no single point at which these will be available, where customs officials can verify their value and quantity.

Developed countries should be forcing the governments of the offshoring countries to bring down trade barriers. India, for example, has very high customs duties for imports and a currency that is not freely convertible. With lowered or eliminated tariffs, US goods will be less expensive for Indians to buy and will thus have a market. A fully convertible currency will allow Indians to buy dollars in the open market with rupees and travel to the US and other countries, giving a boost to their tourism industries.

In a free market, with offshoring increasing, the dollar inflow into India will increase, leading to an appreciation of the rupee, making service exports expensive. To keep offshoring competitive, the Indian government will have to keep the rupee low by buying dollars in the open market. This, however, increases the rupee money supply, which leads to inflation in the country. Not only is inflation politically undesirable, but it also makes offshoring noncompetitive as local salaries and rents increase. Therefore, the only way to keep the rupee low in the face of rising dollar inflows is to bring down trade and currency barriers. This will result in dollars being used for importing foreign goods.

This is already happening in China, where the government may revalue its currency upwards. Anticipating the revaluation, Chinese citizens have been selling US funds in favor of Chinese bonds. Any revaluation of the yuan upwards will increase China's purchasing power. China has been importing raw materials from the US in increasing quantities, creating jobs in America.

The Chinese yuan is pegged at 8.28 to the US dollar and undervalued by up to 30 percent according to several experts. Even though the Chinese government may be unwilling to revalue the currency, market currents may give it no choice. The US Federal Reserve has urged China to revalue its currency. Even the market feels that the yuan must be revalued. In the books of all governments, the section "errors and omissions" shows the flow of underground cross-border money that the governments cannot track. In China, $136 billion flowed out of the country between 1989 and 2001; however, in 2002, an inflow of $7.8 billion showed an expectation that the currency might be revalued. Also US and European central banks are buying yuan assets, and the inflow into China will force a revaluation of the currency. This will make US exports to China more competitive and Chinese imports less competitive.

Bringing down barriers to facilitate free trade is better than erecting new barriers to prevent trade. Not only will levying tariffs on services hurt global trade, but also companies that use offshore services will resist such a move.

Regaining equilibrium in the market

The only other option is to allow market forces to regain equilibrium. The export of processes to low-cost countries means that the US gets goods and services at a much lower cost. It improves the standard of living in the country and creates the possibility of a higher savings rate. The creation of jobs overseas also means wealth generation in the developing countries, increasing their purchasing power, which will eventually lead them to buy goods and services from the US and other developed countries. In fact, China, which manufactures a lot of goods for the US, now imports from the US. It was China that caused the first wave of offshore outsourcing and the subsequent job loss in the US manufacturing sector. The same is expected to happen with the current wave of services outsourcing. The demand from countries like India for US goods will increase US job opportunities to meet that demand. It will also increase global trade, which will spread prosperity.

In India, the increased level of hiring has pushed up salaries by about 20 to 25 percent a year. Some multinational firms offering offshoring services have entered the space late and are offering employees salaries as much as 60 percent higher. For example, a senior level manager in a multinational firm in India can now earn $90,000 to $100,000. This may be lower than salaries in the US, but the 60 to 80 percent salary gap between the compensation of the two countries is now narrowing to 30 or 40 percent. The attrition rate in even tier-1 Indian companies has consequently gone up from about six to ten percent.

As top talent moves to multinational companies for higher salaries and a better brand, Indian companies will have to play catch-up. This will increase the pay of all players in the offshore outsourcing space. The increased competition from multinational players and the stepped-up hiring by Indian outsourcers will keep increasing salaries. TCS, the largest offshore outsourcing company in India, plans to hire 3,000 professionals in 2003, Wipro hired 1,000 professionals in first quarter of 2003, and Cognizant Technology Solutions has proposed to hire nearly 2,000 professionals in the next two years.

Such mid-sized software firms as Polaris, Mascon, and Mascot Systems are recruiting. The employment sections of Indian newspapers are filled with advertisements for software and BPO talent. And such leading multinational firms as IBM Global Systems, EDS, Accenture, PricewaterhouseCoopers, Cap Gemini, and Ernst & Young are hiring more professionals in India.

Accenture plans to increase the number of software professionals to 5,000 by 2004 from 100 in 2001. IBM is building its own facility in Bangalore. CSC and Satyam Computers have formed a joint venture to leverage offshore outsourcing.

Even in the BPO space, companies are hiring. GE had planned to hire 10,000 people by 2005, and this number has been surpassed. Conseco is planning to add two more centers in Noida and Mumbai.

As the demand for labor increases with the entry of new players and more processes being shipped overseas, salaries are bound to increase. This will give India greater purchasing power, enabling its people to buy goods and services from the US and other developed countries. In fact, the National Council of Applied Economic Research in India states that the middle class is expanding, so more and more families can afford to buy white goods and automobiles. Estimates point that about 400 million Indians are now middle class, earning at least $1,800 a year, an increase of 17 percent since 2000. The council expects the number to rise by another 24 percent by 2007.

As a result, foreign companies have started setting up operations in India and are growing successfully. They include such automobile manufacturers as GM, Ford, Toyota, DaimlerChrysler, and Honda; services like Citibank and McDonald's; and other manufacturers like Motorola, Reebok, and Nokia. Citibank is getting new customers: The average age of a Citibank mortgage holder in India used to be 41; now it's 28. Pizza Hut plans to open 100 restaurants in India over the next two years to add to its current 50. Domino's plans to add a dozen of outlets annually to its 90 outlets. Motorola's sales of mobile phones in India increased 200 percent in the first six months of 2003 over the same period the previous year. Sales of Reebok footwear are growing by 30 percent a year, media reports state.

The market eventually finds its equilibrium and it is best if governments let them function uninterrupted.

Case Studies

The ABN AMRO Bank Story

ABN AMRO Bank has over 3,594 branches in more than 74 countries, a staff of 110,000 employees, and assets of €543 billion (as of December 2002). It is listed on several stock exchanges, including Amsterdam, London, and New York. The bank focuses on three client segments: consumer and commercial clients (CCC), private clients and asset management (PCAM), and wholesale clients (WC).

The CCC unit services individuals and small to medium enterprises requiring day-to-day banking. The bank offers CCC services mainly through its presence in three home markets: the US Midwest, the Netherlands, and Brazil. This unit's new growth markets division is expanding its consumer and commercial operations in such countries as India and greater China.

The PCAM group caters to individuals and institutional investors. ABN AMRO is a leading player in private banking in both the Netherlands and France, and has strong positions in Luxembourg, Switzerland, and Miami. The private clients segment ranks among the world's top 10, with €96 billion in assets under administration; the asset management segment has a local presence in 30 countries and €150 billion in assets under management.

The WC unit provides services to major international corporations and institutions. One of the largest Europe-based wholesale banking businesses, it has 20,000 staff and operations in over 40 countries. With a global network, specialists in all major industry sectors, and a broad range of products, ABN AMRO provides local and global expertise for complex cross-border deals.

Before dividing the bank into three distinct units, ABN AMRO had a geographic focus. By changing the strategic focus from geographic to client-centered operations, the stage was set for offshore BPO. ABN AMRO had shared services companies running in North America and the Netherlands, and set up a third one in India.

The imperative

"The business case for a fully owned BPO entity in India was justified by the cost savings from India alone," says Meera Sanyal, managing director of ABN AMRO central enterprise services

(ACES). The cost advantages multiply if business processes are insourced from the network, as the cost of hiring talent in India is much lower than hiring the same talent in the US or Europe.

There is also the advantage of scale, as India has a large pipeline of educated people, with universities turning out nearly 300,000 graduates a year. With such a huge workforce, an entry-level processor can be hired for as little as 10,000 rupees (about $250) a month. The cost and availability of talent was just one of ABN AMRO's reasons to move processes to India; the quality of talent was the other.

The Indian banking sector has been undergoing a shakeout since the late 1990s. Several experienced bankers have opted for voluntary retirement schemes (VRS) of various public-sector banks. Says Sanyal: "India has a wealth of world-class knowledge in the banking area, several of whom are looking for alternative opportunities post the VRS in nationalized banks." This talent can be used to good purpose for quality assurance on banking operations. The cost and talent access were important reasons for ABN AMRO to consider moving its business processes to India.

ABN AMRO's strong rationale to move to India was explained recently by a top official of the bank. Speaking at the opening of the Mumbai hub, Dolf Collee, member of the managing board, ABN AMRO Bank N.V. said: "India provides the right mix of efficient, good-quality English speaking population which enables us to provide high quality, cost-effective IT enabled services to ABN AMRO Bank worldwide."

Romesh Sobti, executive vice president and country representative, ABN AMRO Bank, India added: "India is fast emerging as a major hub for IT enabled services. This is one more affirmation on the capabilities of the Indian workforce. ACES is driven by the objective of lowering the cost of processing of services for the ABN AMRO Bank in India and elsewhere." According to Sanyal, ACES should be able to reduce the total cost of process ownership by 40 to 70 percent by insourcing offshore to India, depending on the nature and complexity of the process.

The steps to offshoring

How did ABN AMRO get into India? First, they found that competitors like Citibank and Standard Chartered Bank were also insourcing business processes to India. They used this fact to sell the idea of offshore insourcing internally.

Also the cost benefit strongly justified the business case for offshore outsourcing. Since India had the benefit of scale, ABN AMRO decided to set up a shared services company in India to deal with processing. Says Sanyal: "We initially decided to establish services in India to assist ABN AMRO's Indian operations." This is now being scaled to take on tasks from other units worldwide.

To provide these services, ABN AMRO created ACES as a subsidiary in 2001. In 2002, ABN AMRO initiated BPO through ACES to serve the Indian operations. However, the success of the venture spread rapidly through its close-knit global network, and several divisions began asking for the services. By early 2002, ACES moved to its second phase, offering services to the global operations of ABN AMRO for trade operations and cash payments from Chennai. A second hub was set up in Mumbai with 401 seats working three eight-hour shifts; an expansion plan will soon double this capacity.

ABN AMRO chose Mumbai on the recommendation of Arthur Andersen, an independent consultant, as it could provide a robust infrastructure and a good supply of power and excellent telecommunication facilities. It also had a strong and reliable public transport system for the staff working on a 24/7 basis. The only problem was Mumbai's relatively high cost of premises. ABN AMRO found a 33,000-square-foot Mumbai location in a defunct textile mill in Parel, offering both a reasonable price of real estate and excellent transport facilities. The bank invested about €2 million to set up the hub.

The Mumbai hub is the main center for processing banking operations outside of trade and cash. It is also the main IT hub that acts as the gateway for offshore application development and maintenance services. For example, ACES provides application support for cash management systems to 13 Asia Pacific countries and global support for the security documentation system to 30 countries. The Chennai hub provides global trade and advisory and cash management services. The bank has another hub in New Delhi to service the centralized consumer operations. The three hubs provide disaster recovery to each other.

ACES is run as a cost center. Sanyal says: "Our shared services center in India has been set up with the objective of lowering the total cost of ownership of systems and processes to ABN AMRO business units worldwide." Its main objective is to reduce costs, not make profits. Hence, ACES is judged and rewarded as a cost center. Its benefit is tangible revenue saving, which is tracked and measured.

Part of the ABN AMRO decision to set up BPO operations in India was that the services would be performed by a subsidiary and not the bank itself. This was desirable fiscally due to the tax holiday on the export of services and transfer pricing regulations, in addition to the difference in salaries between bank staff and employees working at BPO centers.

ABN AMRO decided to keep BPO operations under its umbrella as these were mission-critical. Before ACES, an external vendor provided call center services for ABN AMRO India; once the subsidiary was formed, the bank insourced the activity even though the cost increased somewhat. The strongest reason for insourcing the service was to reduce the operational risks associated with a third-party vendor and to improve quality of service to customers. With outsourcing, the bank had little control on the vendor employees, and the attrition rates eventually affected its customer service standards.

In day-to-day operations, business unit (BU) heads of ACES have both onshore and offshore targets set in productivity, costs, and so on. Service level agreements (SLAs) are entered into by ACES with each client BU. This means that ACES unit heads have a target and so does the process owner. The SLAs specify roles and responsibilities both of the customer and the ACES department serving them as well as its deliverables: IT availability and uptime; ATM guaranteed uptime and processing times; accounts payable turnaround times; and call center pick times and dropped calls. ACES sets benchmarks for the processes it runs, which makes it easy to monitor deliverables against the SLAs. Six Sigma quality methods are applied to continuously improve performance.

ACES uses a transfer pricing mechanism and bills customers after adding a markup on cost as required by the India transfer pricing regulations. The books of ACES are open to its customers and give clear visibility into the costs. Says Sanyal: "Operating as a cost center, it is critical that this is a very transparent mechanism."

And since comparable market pricing is not available, ACES invites its internal clients to go to other BPO service providers and get quotes to see if ACES is competitive. This increases the comfort level of internal customers. In fact, before deciding to transfer any processing activity to ACES, ABN AMRO conducted a thorough analysis of the benefits and costs of insourcing versus outsourcing to a third party. By ABN AMRO's rule book, ACES must pass the acid test of "make vs. buy" each time a process has to be moved, which ensures that both shareholder value and client satisfaction are maximized.

The processes offshored

A key reason to send non-core processes offshore is to enable companies to excel in core activities. ACES has adhered to this principle, even in the kind of work it takes on. ACES provides services in information, communication and technology, transaction services for a banking operations, and call centers. It decided to not set up offshore development centers for software development, as "this is not our core competency and if we need IT development we will go to a software services company."

However, ACES acts as a gateway for ABN AMRO for software outsourcing process. It helps the bank's units select Indian software vendors and assists with project management to assure quality. Once the software development work is done, ACES can also step in during the maintenance phase of the software's lifecycle. In a sense, ACES is like IBM or EDS that provides software maintenance and hosting.

Advice

It is easy to show a cost benefit by transferring processes offshore, purely due to the labor cost. "But one must not get carried away by that number," says Sanyal. To make the model sustainable over the long term, it is important to focus on productivity. "Keeping this in mind, we inculcated the work culture based on a demanding customer like ABN AMRO in India." Indians are used to working long hours, thereby enhancing employee productivity.

ACES is careful to meet the quality standards dictated by the ABN AMRO's European culture but also adheres to the Indian work week. "When people are sending processes to India, they should crystallize their expectations both in terms of qualitative and quantitative deliverables which the Indian work ethic is then able to deliver. These vectors should always be in place." This is crucial to the success of any offshore outsourcing initiative to India.

A trend in the offshore BPO space is software companies setting up centers to run business processes. These software companies have exposure to the US markets and are leveraging their existing relationships to win BPO assignments.

Meera Sanyal feels that software companies may not have the quick success they expect in running BPO, as this is a completely different area from development of software services. But she adds that IT companies have robust processes and quality standards, which they can apply to BPO. BPO can learn from the IT experience, but one has to realize it is a different model.

The Citibank Story

Citibank is one of the most technologically advanced banks in the world, having invented and implemented such banking technologies as branch-wide networks of automated teller machines, credit card authorization systems, electronic payments networks, and transaction processing systems.

The bank is also one of the early adopters of offshore outsourcing. Needing to reduce costs and to get scarce IT resources for regional support centers in 1996, Citibank's Latin American Consumer Bank (LACB) decided offshore outsourcing was the way to go.

Technological support for the Latin American operations had been provided from the US, which was expensive. To reduce the cost, Citibank initially brought in a vendor to execute non-critical work. It started looking at a more long-term strategy to reduce costs, improve quality, increase the speed to market, and move to a more robust platform from an old legacy system.

The imperative

Apart from cost, Citibank needed to improve the process quality of its technology centers. Since offshore IT vendors specialize in software engineering, they have better processes, which would benefit the bank. Also shifting processes offshore meant moving to a 24/7 development cycle, which would result in faster delivery of services.

Efrain Jovel, former CIO of Citibank LACB, says: "It was imperative that we go offshore as the IT infrastructure of the Latin American operations had redundant systems and functions, quality of processes and methods were incipient, speed to market was slow and the legacy systems depended on key star performers." Indian software vendors were known to provide quality processes, and "follow the sun" development cycles reduced the time to market.

With its availability of talent, unlike the US, India could provide a fast ramp-up, if required. Also, Citibank could not risk depending on star performers to handle its legacy systems, which emphasized people rather than processes. Through documentation and use of widely accepted programming languages, offshore vendors drastically reduced the dependence on people.

141

The steps to offshoring

In 1998, Citibank's LACB operations wanted to establish a strategy to consolidate ten technology centers to two centers to achieve operational efficiency and cost reduction. The consumer bank had experience working with outside vendors for specific purposes, such as specialized software applications for ATM transaction processing and front-end teller technology, so the transition to an offshore supplier would be smooth. "Way back in 1996 we decided that we needed outside vendors for regional center support," says Jovel.

At a cost of more than $100 million a year, 10 technology centers in Tampa, Fort Lauderdale, Mexico, Puerto Rico, Colombia, Venezuela, Brazil, Peru, Chile, and Argentina served Citibank LACB. In 1998, Citibank consolidated the activities into two centers—in Buenos Aires, Argentina, for the south, and in Monterrey, Mexico, for the north. They reduced the cost of running technology centers by almost 20 percent; however, as Jovel says: "Consolidation alone would not reduce cost at the levels needed, so we also went for offshore outsourcing. The labor arbitrage would bring down the costs by around 20 percent."

The bank also decided that it would outsource computer systems testing functions, 24/7 application support, software development, and maintenance projects, which involved moving from a legacy system to a client-server technology.

To execute the strategy, Citibank LACB invited five firms to bid for the projects; it ended up accepting three. It gave Mascon the 24/7 support project, which was strategic in nature and later became critical. Mascon also had to move the Monterrey AS/400 legacy platform to a more robust client-server technology. As Citibank personnel served as business analysts, the processes within the bank did not experience any interruption during the move. Says Jovel: "Mascon took just six months to understand the technology and they moved the platform and support functions to Monterrey before schedule. As a company they were flexible and had strong communications skills, which lead to the smooth progression of the project."

One project in Puerto Rico was given to Hinduja Group's HTMT; another one in Brazil went to TCS, the largest Indian software services company. Puerto Rico went off well; however, says Jovel "The Brazil project handled by TCS did not end up flying. It is not that TCS did not understand our legacy systems well, but Brazil, after the knowledge transfer period, made a decision to do it internally. Brazilians did not feel comfortable to outsource offshore."

The project execution followed a clearly defined process. In the case of offshore maintenance support, every new development requirement identified by the bank was documented as a technology service request (TSR). Processing TSRs included:

- initiation—receipt of TSR; initial analysis and estimate

- definition—preparation and approval of functional specifications

- design—preparation of high-level design and program specifications

- build—coding and unit testing

- verification—integration testing and user acceptance testing

- implementation—release to production

- post-implementation review—collection of metrics

The offshore development team was largely involved in the design and build phases. The on-site Mascon team was more involved in initiation, definition, verification, and implementation.

The processes offshored

Citibank's LACB outsourced software projects, maintenance, testing, and 24/7 application support. However, it did not outsource business systems analysis, account management, IT strategies, architecture, development life cycle methodology, project management, or new technologies, as these were very close to the bank's core processes.

One outsourced project was the sales and service automation initiative, basically a teller system that handled deposits, withdrawals, loan payments, foreign exchange selling and buying transactions, fund transfers, card payments, and utility payments. The application is multilingual, multi-currency, and multi-location. It exists in all Latin American branches and interacts with a central system, which is on an AS/400 platform that carries the central database for all banking applications. The system, however, is designed to interact as easily with other systems—midrange, mainframe, or client-server platform. Requiring 75 person-years, the development was carried out in Chennai, India.

In the maintenance area, Citibank engaged Mascon to provide ongoing maintenance support. Mascon put a team in Tampa, Florida, to provide on-site support for applications related to their operations at their Latin American headquarters in the areas of business as usual (BAU), production support (PS), and quality assurance (QA). Additionally, a team of AS/400 banking specialists was placed in Chennai to provide offshore support, including enhancements of existing application and development of new applications. This project involved a total of 25 person-years.

In production support, Mascon sent about 20 consultants to Citibank offices for support and maintenance management. Initially, the consultants were trained in Tampa and later sent to Chennai and Monterrey to provide off-site support. The support activity was mission-critical to the bank.

Benefits

Citibank LACB was able to get a 30 percent cost reduction through consolidation and offshoring. The initial benefit from outsourcing was $6 million, but this rapidly increased as more processes were moved offshore. In fact, outsourcing applications development, maintenance, and support of Citibank LACB's northern regional support center alone saved 35 percent of operating expenses. Another major benefit was the significant reduction in middle management overhead and training expenses required to keep technology centers running with new technologies.

Moving processes offshore enabled Citibank's technology centers to focus on new areas. Says Jovel: "We needed a strategic offshore partner to take care of the legacy work, while the internal Citibank resources were allocated to support and develop new systems to launch new products and services. Prior to offshore outsourcing, Citibank was not able to focus on new technologies as day-to-day legacy work was taking away all resources."

Once the offshore vendor entered Citibank, only a few of the bank's key resources were left in charge of managing the requirements of the legacy work, and the rest were re-allocated to support the strategy that implemented new technologies in data warehousing, customer relationship management, and Internet and intranet banking.

"The offshoring exercise resulted in a dramatic improvement in the delivery of software," says Jovel. Citibank was quickly able to implement touch-point technologies in call centers and branch automation arenas and significantly enhance the core banking software with multi-currency and risk management capabilities. Jovel adds that the bank improved services to levels that would have been very difficult, if not impossible, if executed internally. "We were meeting response times and budget targets at a rate of 98 to 99.5 percent."

Citibank also made a marked improvement in service quality after offshoring by signing tight service level agreements. "We had several quality improvements like reduction in response time to maintenance reports and quotations for fixes, production error reductions in systems developed, among others."

The bank benefited in training and from the use of cutting edge tools and methodology in software development. The offshore vendors had excellent project tracking tools, which gave Citibank full visibility into the software development process. Says Jovel: "After offshoring, Citibank's technology centers were able to focus on core-business processes and products, concentrate on client needs versus technology itself, lower cost, improve quality, improve customer satisfaction and increase Citibank's reliability on IT."

Jovel feels that he should have pushed for assigning more offshore resources to reduce cost. "We never got to the level of offshoring that we wanted," he says. Citibank had a number of Indian consultants on-site, which gave it more control and made it easier to ensure service quality, but this also eroded the cost benefit. "The trick is to find a formula to balance offshore and on-site resources, with on-site resources kept to the minimum. Simultaneously, strong control mechanisms should be in place to ensure offshore quality and service levels."

It is necessary to have a good tracking tool for assigning resources to projects. As resources move between on-site to offshore locations or are re-assigned to other projects, it is important to maintain control of their activities and use. "The tracking tool of the vendor must send alerts on the client's dashboard as changes in resources have a major impact on costs and productivity."

Advice

Citibank LACB chose India, as the pricing was much better than other countries. Indian companies also have a consistent software development methodology and quality certifications. "Compared to the Philippines and other Eastern European service providers, India ranks higher on professional and intellectual parameters," says Jovel.

Latin American countries are worth examining for their proximity to the US, but in most cases, they do not offer the cost, skills, and productivity advantages of India. Citibank actually moved Indian resources to work on Latin American on-site projects. This took care of the skill shortage issue, but it was still more expensive than developing programs in India. Although it is less expensive than India, Brazil is subject to currency devaluation; thus, maintaining stability in unit costs becomes difficult.

Jovel feels that companies will start looking at Latin America for offshore outsourcing, as Asia will not be able to support future exponential growth in the area, although it must be ready to manage more immature sources of software engineering activities.

The Infosys-Progeon Story

Infosys Technologies Limited is a consulting and IT services company. Although it started operations in 1981, Infosys had only 12 clients and 300 employees in 1992. Then, according to Sudarshan Narasimhamurthy, alliance manager at Infosys: "From 1992 to 2003, revenues grew from about $4 million to $753 million, and the number of clients increased to over 300."

In the 1980s, Infosys was a programming shop and still new to play the role as an end-to-end service provider. It did the bulk of software development on-site at clients' facilities. With the liberalization of the Indian economy, the telecom infrastructure links began to improve in the early 1990s and companies were enabled to raise capital from the markets. Thus, world-class offshore development centers could be established in India with good communication links to their international clients. This was when the offshoring activities picked up steam. Today, continuously going up the value chain, Infosys has entered the business process outsourcing space by leveraging its existing client relationships.

Software processes

Infosys exports software processes offshore to provide value, quality, and cost-effective solutions to its clients. Its global delivery model (GDM) provides quick ramp-up, training, robust project management, and quality processes. "By taking over the process, Infosys converts fixed costs to variable costs, in addition to providing absolute cost savings," says Narasimhamurthy.

How

The Infosys GDM aims at exporting work to locations where it can best be executed both cost-effectively and with minimal amount of risk. In the GDM framework, the engagement teams scattered geographically are perfectly co-ordinated through seamless communication and clearly defined process guidelines. The GDM delivers services from several locations through a networked environment aimed at recoverability. One location or development center serves as a back-up for another, ensuring complete redundancy.

To meet short development cycles, the GDM offers extended workdays across multiple time zones for faster engagement completion. Infosys divides engagements into work pieces executed independently and simultaneously at global development centers, resulting in faster time-to-market. Engagements have two characteristic components: The on-site parts are executed at the client site where they can receive close client interaction, proximity to the market, and quick turnaround times; the offshore component, executed at a remote location, covers activities that are scalable and research oriented and can be executed without constant interaction with end-users or clients.

Infosys decides the distribution of activities based on the specific requirements of an engagement. Some activities are run simultaneously, with teams from both locations providing complementary skills. Some factors that decide the distribution of activities between on-site and remote locations are the availability of skill sets, the client's need to be in control, the amount of risk mitigation required, cost implications, and the amount of work involved.

Infosys typically executes these functions on-site: analysis and planning; high-level design; and user interface design, project co-ordination, on-site testing, implementation, and rapid reaction support in the post implementation phase. These tasks usually define the scope and direction of the overall engagement and signal the successful closure of engagements. The key resources work with the client management and end-users at client sites. They are assisted by research and inputs from remote support teams, based on requirements.

Infosys typically executes these functions offshore: project management, detailed design and build, documentation, warranty support, and maintenance. Offshore work usually involves the bulk of the engagement execution and needs processes, tools, and systems for an efficient and predictable execution. Here, productivity is improved by knowledge management and the use of standardized methodologies, systems, and tools.

To deliver world-class solutions, Infosys has adopted CMM Integration (CMMI) level 5 procedures into its GDM. The GDM also provides for a seamless flow of information and access to experts and knowledge bases at multiple sites, which allows monitoring, tracking, and quickly reacting to changing requirements and scaling up. Because scaling is a critical success factor for many IT engagements, the GDM offers access to expert and infrastructure resources at multiple locations, ensuring quick ramp-ups and high scalability. Infosys is a certified CMMI level 5 organization, the highest SEI level. Engagement teams perform various activities, as part of the CMMI level 5 compliance, to deliver high-quality solutions in a predictable fashion.

At the engagement-planning phase, Infosys defines quality goals and parameters based on metrics derived from its experiences. To meet the unique requirements of each engagement, Infosys refines these parameters with their variance limits set in advance, tracks these quality goals and parameters on an ongoing basis for variance, and corrects any variance beyond the defined threshold. To reach the highest levels of quality and to prevent variance, the engagement execution process includes multiple levels of review.

Integrated tools and systems ensure that remote teams interact seamlessly to guarantee quality work. An independent quality group also periodically monitors and audits the engagement. For further risk mitigation, senior management regularly reviews key focus areas of the engagement.

Once a client opts for the GDM, an IT function moves from an approach based on resources, activities, or micro-management to one based on deliverables or SLA-based engagement management, that is, from physical to virtual control. The engagement control is transferred to a joint management council that has members of both Infosys and the client to ensure that the right mix of services is executed at the right time to leverage GDM and achieve economies of scale.

The GDM has mechanisms to keep clients informed about all engagement-related activities at remote locations. At the engagement-planning phase, all aspects are covered and a detailed schedule is created, which is shared and discussed with the client engagement manager. This person is also updated through regular status report meetings, at which the progress of the engagement is reviewed against the plan and any necessary changes are made to the plan and schedule. This meeting is also used to highlight all high-priority open issues. Some engagements also have a steering committee comprising senior management from both the client and Infosys to review progress.

A team under the GDM is built so that the client has minimal need to interact with the remote team. The engagement team is headed by a resident engagement manager at the client site to co-ordinate all its activities with the remote team offshore. The on-site team directly communicates with the remote teams on such issues as requirement changes, design reviews, change request sign-offs, clarifications, and issue resolutions. This team also handles all client interactions that require immediate resolution and quick turnaround.

The GDM can address changing requirements and ensures quick turnarounds. For engagements with evolving requirements, the design and prototyping teams work from development centers located close to the client, in Fremont, Boston, Toronto, New Jersey, Chicago, Tokyo, and London. As the Infosys team and the client are based in the same or near time zones, close interaction during this critical phase is possible. Once the requirements are frozen, development work is distributed between the on-site and remote development centers to ensure availability of the right people at the right time to respond quickly to the immediate needs of the engagement.

When requirements are expected to change continuously, key members of the Infosys on-site team form a part of the core client team to review changes. Team members identify priorities, evaluate downstream impact, and ensure immediate communication with remote teams. Along with a strong ability to trace requirements and change management processes, this approach ensures quick and effective response to changing requirements.

In the IT world, applications may be incompatible and require different hardware and software platforms. The GDM infrastructure addresses the hardware and software requirements of most applications. But some unique integration needs for unsupported hardware, software platforms, and beta versions of software and complex deployment platforms are addressed through a variety of mechanisms.

Infosys operates from eight cities in India, which can collectively house 18,800 people. The connectivity between the remote locations of Infosys and client sites is set up using well-established and proven models that ensure a high level of security and redundancy. The Infosys communications network is a worldwide area network, which links all major offices to provide data, voice, and video communication.

The links (with built-in redundancy) enable Infosys to provide cost-effective maintenance and co-development of software as well as an effective medium for e-mail and video conferencing with clients. Infosys has a mix of leased and ISDN circuits that connect development centers in India with its headquarters in Bangalore. There is a redundant power supply backed by UPS, switched high bandwidth LAN, several high-speed communication links on satellite and fiber, and overseas network hubs in the US, Canada, Europe, and Asia Pacific. Moreover, Infosys has dedicated 24/7 network management teams to ensure uninterrupted client connectivity.

Infosys has global HR policies with high standards of recruitment to ensure a group of highly motivated people with complementary skills. It has a culture of teamwork, transparency, and client orientation that transcends geographical boundaries. Along with a world-class infrastructure, Infosys has mature quality processes and a quality-focused workforce in a distributed environment. In addition, multiple locations minimize risk and provide necessary flexibility to ramp up.

In the two decades that the GDM has been in existence, Infosys has refined and built a world-class delivery model. Infosys states that its people, processes, and infrastructure make a significant difference in providing the best solution with the least amount of risk to clients.

Adding BPO

To extend its services and to meet the demand from existing clients, Infosys set up Progeon, its BPO subsidiary. Says Subrat Mohanty, head of solutions design at Progeon: "Lots of Infosys clients kept asking for a BPO service which led to the formation of Progeon." Progeon is a separate company, whose line workers are graduates, not software engineers as in Infosys, and it follows a different wage structure.

Using its GDM, its core competency, Infosys entered the BPO space. "GDM takes one whole process and breaks it into pieces and finds the most economic way and geography to deliver the pieces." According to Mohanty: "Entering BPO is not moving away from IT space. One needs domain expertise to execute processes, but also needs an IT grounding on which these processes run. From the customer's point of view, Infosys provides seamless maintenance of IT and business processes."

The BPO space is traditionally either the voice or data business. "Progeon works on a different premise. The client is at the center of the strategy and the company will take whatever the client wants to outsource." In the vertical space, Progeon focuses on financial services and telecom. In the horizontal area, it focuses on finance and accounting, HR and administration, customer service, sales order processes, mortgage services, and reconciliation.

Progeon helps clients decrease costs by exporting business processes, most of which are labor intensive and take up precious management time. This enables the client to focus on core functions rather than processes that do not add value or create an edge in the market. And the fact that back-office to the client is the front-office to Progeon leads to quick process improvements and development of best practices.

BPO is executed in three steps: discovery, transition, and execution. Either Progeon or the client company can complete the first phase, in which it discovers which processes can be outsourced by putting them in a 2×2 grid to measure "fitness to offshore" and risk. In the discovery phase, Progeon looks at such factors as number of people, whether the process is core, and process inefficiencies. Under risk, it looks at such factors as interdependence of processes with core processes, confidential data, and interaction with customer.

In the transition phase, Progeon develops a plan for transition, executes knowledge and technology transfer, and puts metrics in place to measure performance. Then it ramps down functions on-site and ramps them up offshore. In the execution phase, Progeon decides how to run everyday processes, work the logistics, measure defects and productivity, and concentrate on manpower issues and training.

Progeon can reduce a company's BPO cost by 35 to 50 percent and can offer productivity and quality gains. The extent of benefits depends on the customer's current locations, degree of automation, and internal efficiencies. Progeon measures the cost benefit at a transactional level, unlike several other vendors that provide numbers based on labor arbitrage alone.

"At one of our customer's, Progeon looked at the total costs of servicing a loan to baseline costs," says Mohanty. Many clients do not know their baseline cost, so they ask to export the process first and check cost savings later. Most of the cost calculations are effort based and not transaction based. In BPO, 60 to 70 percent of the cost is related to telecommunication and infrastructure, and this can be spread out by increased use by all customers.

Progeon tells its customers not to outsource time-critical and non-standard process and also to communicate change to all stakeholders.

Where

Mohanty says that the Philippines has the English-language advantage but is limited by the small number of graduates available to run BPO. The demand for high-quality labor would keep increasing, and the cost advantages might not be sustainable in the long run. China has the graduates, but English-language ability restricts its potential for some time. In the meantime, India, with its English-language advantage, graduates over two million annually, and the labor cost arbitrage advantage in India will be sustainable.

Other countries could emerge to provide services to non-English-speaking companies—Indonesia for Dutch-speaking and Mauritius for French-speaking counties. These countries could occupy niche positions and serve customers as effectively as India.

The Mascon Story

Mascon is a $60 million, ISO 9001-certified and CMM assessed global provider of IT services and, according to Deloitte Touche Tohmatsu, the fastest growing technology company in Chicago in 2002. Mascon employs over 1,200 IT professionals at offshore software development and maintenance centers in India and at on-site software and business development offices in Mexico, the UK, and the US.

Through an innovative blend of products, services, and delivery models, Mascon assists companies in building, deploying, and maintaining technology-based solutions in their business strategy. Its on-site/offshore delivery method has provided its clients the speed, scale, and cost advantage necessary to thrive in a competitive economy. Mascon's partners include such industry leaders as GE (manufacturing), Northern Trust (banking), Lucent & UTStarcom (telecommunications), Walgreens (retail), AGT (digital asset management), and MGIC (insurance). Technology practices spanning multiple verticals are Mascon's core competencies, allowing it to deliver solutions at the application level (e.g., e-business, enterprise applications) and at an infrastructure level (e.g., communications technology, embedded systems).

Mascon also provides BPO services through a partnership with, Antares Publishing Services (Antares). Mascon and Antares jointly tap the existing client base of Mascon with a view to provide value added services. "Pressure to reduce costs, improve efficiency and increase flexibility in the back office seem to be driving many of our clients to request us to extend BPO services" says R Gowri Shanker, Managing Partner at Mascon. The alliance will cover all aspects of BPO, including customer contact services, pay roll services, claims processing and billing services, tailor-made to suit the requirements of individual corporate.

How does this offshore service provider deliver processes to its clients? First, every step of Mascon's offshore outsourcing process is managed professionally. The vendor has back-ups to ensure recoverability, quality processes to deliver bug-free software code, and seamless operations. Mascon works closely with its clients in a partnership that aims to deliver customer satisfaction. The most crucial elements contributing to the maturity of the offshore delivery model are Mascon's understanding of the process and the control mechanisms.

Mascon has built its delivery model and institutionalized the required skills from years of executing projects at organizations of varying sizes, in different industries, and in numerous locations. The company has delivery processes for such functions as software development, testing, and application management outsourcing. The delivery model of application management outsourcing gives good insight into the maturity of Mascon's processes.

The key processes for setting up an outsourcing engagement include team building, infrastructure building, planning, on-site knowledge acquisition, off-site training and transition, and outsourcing. For the successful set-up and operation of an outsourcing engagement, Mascon works on these elements: physical location and infrastructure; hardware and software infrastructure; security and confidentiality; transition management; project management; remote communication; and quality management.

Personnel identification

Mascon believes that the success of any significant technology development project is rooted in management commitment. Therefore, it encourages business ownership of the project and its ultimate outcome. An account manager is assigned as the business owner with overall responsibility to the project. That person works with the client's outsourcing program manager, the contact for the business relationship, to arrive at the resource and project needs. The two are key to the success of the outsourcing relationship.

To make services seamless and risk free, Mascon appoints an on-site technical project manager to co-ordinate and ensure delivery of the development components of the software system. Mascon's on-site team ensures that the client need not worry about the logistics of using a remote software development facility.

Knowledge acquisition

Knowledge acquisition and transfer is part of a 12-week, structured, four-stage process for transferring application maintenance from the client's internal IT staff to the Mascon team. The functional, technical, and maintenance process study phases normally happen during the first six weeks. The remaining six weeks are the offshore transition phase when the two organizations' teams work together through the maintenance process to get the required hands-on experience. A group of key Mascon consultants posted at the client's site gather knowledge on the application and then document the findings.

In the functional study, the team: learns the functionality of the applications and prioritizes them based on the client's business model; maps the business functions to programs and data sources; generates process flows; documents user profile; and studies error history to identify key system problem areas.

The technical study includes: documenting the system environment factors, including transaction volume, batch windows, and available test beds; security and access control procedures; maintenance practices; error-resolution process; and training requirements.

The maintenance process study comprises: documenting the processes triggered by error reports or enhancement requests; tracking all events through the entire fix/develop cycle; identifying all tools used and learning the client's change control procedures and error classification schemes; leveraging past experiences in executing application maintenance solutions; and preparing a draft version of maintenance plan that fits the client's requirement.

Transition phase

Mascon executes the identified project based on the approved statement of work. It then prepares a software requirements document and a detailed design document for the proposed work. The execution of the project follows the Mascon project process and quality control life cycle.

The software development processes include extensive reviews and continuous process improvements. Over the years, Mascon has mastered project planning, execution, measurement, escalation, and control. The completion of the project is signified by the delivery of quality software with well-documented source code and instructions. During this phase, Mascon prepares a gap analysis to identify areas requiring future work, completes first level of knowledge repository, defines an application outsourcing road map, and defines the process for release and configuration management.

Outsourced phase

The Mascon account manager has multiple project managers to handle the different projects with the client. Maintenance services are long-term engagements capitalizing on Mascon's offshore maintenance center concept to deliver application maintenance, consisting of: bug fixing; pre-emptive, long-term resolution of production problems; service request processing; enhancements and modifications; application and maintenance documentation; production implementation; 24/7 support or helpdesk; change request management; and root cause analysis.

Infrastructure

At the offshore center, each employee has a workstation/PC, telephone extension, and adequate storage space. The center also has a reception-lounge area, conference rooms, computer room, communications control room, and library. Every engineer at Mascon is equipped with a desktop workstation and software like MS Office. The client arranges or pays for any special hardware or software, which is imported duty free through Software Technology Park and Indian Customs.

Mascon uses the Web to virtually bring the offshore development facility right to the client's site. To ensure maximum benefits from the offshore development center, the company recommends setting up high-speed links to the client's location, with the bandwidth based on the volume of the work. For lower network traffic requirements, the connectivity is through Internet or ISDN dial-up.

Security and confidentiality

Access to the offshore facilities is restricted to personnel associated with the outsourcing engagement. All Mascon facilities are provided with security guards and electronic entry control systems to restrict access to personnel with authorized identification badges. Network security is achieved either by isolating the LAN segment or by implementing firewalls, decided in consultation with the client. In addition, Mascon and the client choose the network access and security guidelines before the start of the outsourcing contract.

All personnel are expected to adhere to the intellectual property protection guidelines. Whenever required, personnel working on an outsourcing engagement adhere to the security guidelines provided by the client. Information confidentiality is maintained through non-disclosure agreements.

Project management

Mascon uses a project management tool called SMART (software methodology and application rollout toolkit), which helps it to follow industry-standard quality processes meticulously. SMART consists of key procedures that must be followed to: achieve project success; deliver software solutions that meet requirements; set and achieve organizational quality objectives; acquire or supply software and services to and from third parties; and operate and maintain software solutions in a production environment. It also includes descriptions and templates for all the key deliverables, including plans, specifications, and forms, as well as checklists that can be used to make sure all procedures are followed correctly.

SMART has a management process guide and a software development process guide to ensure that project delivery from multiple locations adheres to the same standards. These guides reside on a Web server and are accessible by any employee anywhere. The management process guide aids in business planning, project initiation, project planning, project execution, and project close-out. The software development process guide assists in product engineering, release, and supporting activities.

Quality

Says M. Srinivasan, managing partner at Mascon: "We will build a long-term, mutually beneficial relationship with all our customers by ensuring timely delivery of quality software and services, using innovative and continuously improving processes".

The first quality milestone for Mascon was its ISO 9001 certificate awarded by KPMG Quality Registrars in 1996 after assessment of its software development centers at Chennai and Chicago. The certification audit reported zero non-conformances at both the locations. Mascon has established and maintains a documented Mascon quality system (MQS) to ensure that software and services conform to specified requirements. This consists of a quality manual, process handbooks, a procedure manual, standards and guidelines, and quality records like project quality plans.

Mascon's MQS covers all key process areas that affect the software quality directly or indirectly (e.g., software lifecycle activities, supporting activities like purchasing, training, recruitment, induction, performance appraisal, assets management). All MQS documents are maintained under change control. A user-friendly browser-based version of the MQS is accessible to all associates on the Mascon intranet.

Each quality initiative at Mascon is planned, and responsibility for each task is clearly defined. Initiatives include: MQS review; training for all employees; MQS implementation; periodic internal audits and gap analysis to check compliance of MQS by projects and support groups; continuous process improvements; periodic management reviews; external assessments or certifications; and commitment and buy-in from all employees.

Mascon employees at all levels are involved in the process improvement initiative as members of an in-house software engineering process group (SEPG) and process work groups. Processes are revised based on suggestions from employees across the organization. The steering committee is a senior management body chaired by the CEO and comprising all group and software development center heads. It meets every month to oversee implementation of MQS in groups and projects. It also handles all issues related to inter-group co-ordination. This ensures continuous process evaluation and improvement of offshore delivery. This group also evaluates metrics data from projects and support groups and uses this for setting baselines and goals for process performance.

Mascon emphasizes continuous process improvements, based on suggestions from employees, findings, and analysis of internal quality audit and analysis of metrics data from across the organization. All processes at Mascon are institutionalized across the organization, though the projects can tailor these to their specific needs in consultation with the SEPG.

A site-protector database is maintained for all Mascon facilities to disseminate learning from each project across the organization. It includes: metrics for all projects; MQS available to all associates on the intranet as well as on the file server; and a projects repository, which contains project plans, estimation documents, project completion reports, deal-review documents, and a change-request register of all ongoing and closed projects.

Mascon conducts monthly internal quality audits to check compliance with the documented MQS. It investigates the causes of the non-conformance and takes suitable corrective or preventive actions. These have been a major source of process improvements. Mascon also uses external assessments to gain insight into the status of process improvement initiatives and to help benchmark itself with other companies.

Customer satisfaction

Mascon carries out a weekly procedure for each client that tracks the level of customer satisfaction, documenting this process internally against set benchmarks. If feedback is negative, Mascon holds formal meetings with the client, where the problem issue is detailed and the mitigation plans prepared.

Mascon emphasizes metrics collection and analysis for process improvement. It collects metrics data through weekly management status reports for various projects. This analysis and findings lead to process improvements and become a tool for setting goals for the organization and putting in place new processes.

Before project kick-off, a steering committee, consisting of the Mascon project management team and the client team is formed. This committee sets measurable goals and measurement parameters for client's satisfaction. These parameters vary between projects. Some factors the company looks at when measuring customer satisfaction are: ease of approachability and compatibility; ease of understandability; product quality and functionality; quality of effectiveness of project team (both pre- and post-implementation); quality and effectiveness of technical support and customer service; quality and effectiveness of professional services (administrative, consulting, training, mentoring); overall performance of project team; and professionalism of staff. These are graded on a scale of 1 to 5 and then evaluated on a weighted basis to gauge customer satisfaction.

The General Electric Story

Offshore outsourcing was inevitable in General Electric. All the elements were in place, and it was just a matter of time before the offshore initiative achieved scale. The GE culture of speed, boundarylessness, and stretch, and its focus on productivity and quality created path-breaking ways of running a business.

GE leads the way in offshore outsourcing. The $125 billion diversified technology and services company creates products ranging from aircraft engines and power generation to financial services, medical imaging, television programming, and plastics. Experienced in operating from geographically scattered locations, outsourcing IT and business processes offshore was just the right thing to do for GE. The conglomerate operates in over 100 countries and employs more than 300,000 people.

Most of the units of GE have some exposure to the offshore IT development and BPO space, including GE's capital businesses, GE Industrial Systems, and GE Medical Systems. The most notable globalization initiative is the John F. Welch Technology Center (JFWTC) in Bangalore, India, which conducts leading-edge R&D for GE businesses worldwide and has a global presence in India, China, Germany, and the US.

GE's tentative moves to offshore outsourcing in India began in 1994 with software development. Says Scott Bayman, president and CEO, GE India: "We were doing some low-cost software outsourcing before the fall of 1994. Jack Welch visited India that year." After the visit, Welch had a vision that India could be a major destination for exporting software development functions, leading to more complex processes moving offshore. By 1995, GE decided to source intellectual capital from India mostly in the development and maintenance of operational software. In his book, *Straight from the Gut*, Welch says: "I was optimistic about the country's brainpower but our use of it has far outpaced my wildest dreams. The scientific and technical talent in India to do software development, design work and basic research is incredible."

In 1995, GE offshored about $10 million worth of software development and maintenance to India, mostly from GE Appliances, GE Aircraft Engines, and GE Medical Systems. However, Gary Riener, CIO of GE, felt that offshore outsourcing could be much bigger. He, Bayman, and Welch reviewed the progress of GE's offshore initiative regularly. "Top management buy-in is critical for the success of any offshore outsourcing initiative," says Alan Kocsi, director of GE's global development centers (GDCs). After getting the go-ahead from Welch, the GE business unit CIOs projected the existing $10 million volume could be doubled in three years. Then the goal was stretched to $40 million. Says Kocsi: "The ramp-up was amazing. We blew past the three-year stretch goal, achieving $46 million in our first year." GE was contributing about six to eight percent of Indian IT exports at that point.

GE's first big step in offshore outsourcing was setting up GDCs in India. These centers are owned and run by Indian suppliers but provide services exclusively to GE. In 1995, three companies set up dedicated centers for GE in Bangalore and Mumbai to support its worldwide software requirements, and GE shed the cumbersome process of dealing with multiple suppliers engaged on a project-by-project basis. After the software offshoring initiative, GE set up the JFWTC in Bangalore to carry out high-end R&D, with a team working in close collaboration with its counterparts in the US. This is certainly proof that high-end technology and innovation can be worked on from offshore locations.

BPO created a huge impact in GE and was last on the offshoring list. BPO services are provided by GECIS, an Indian unit of GE, which now has more than 10,000 seats. Given the success of BPO in India, GECIS, headed by a GE officer, Pramod Bhasin, opened centers in China and is looking at other locations to cater to non-English- speaking countries in Europe. Setting up a BPO unit in India was Bhasin's idea that was backed by Nigel Andrews, a former senior president of GE Capital. Says Bhasin: "We initially wanted to start small." However, after listening to the idea for about 15 minutes, Andrews felt that scope of BPO was much larger and gave Bhasin the go-ahead. After a few successes, Welch began showcasing the achievements at leadership meets.

Initially, there was resistance to sending business processes offshore. However, showcasing success stories changed the mind-set. Says Bayman: "Initially, GE managers said it can't be done in India but after seeing the success stories, processes move almost automatically to India. Offshore outsourcing has gone beyond expectations and the concept has been well accepted in the GE universe."

GE culture—a strong foundation

When companies grow as fast as GE, they tend to build walls, stifle creativity, waste time, and narrow vision, all of which eventually hinder progress. GE's principle of boundarylessness facilitates the free flow of ideas and improves activity. This concept is manifested in the meeting of employees known as the "Workout," in which people in each department get together to investigate business issues and examine the quickest and simplest ways to move forward. The goal is continuous improvement of processes by comparing them with the excellent methods adopted in other departments or other GE business companies worldwide.

Boundarylessness at GE also enables the optimum integration of all essential resources within the organization and linkage with relevant outside resources. The free flow of creative ideas across all boundaries is essential for innovation. The boundaryless organization transcends hierarchy for hierarchy's sake and rises above isolation by functions or by geography. Everybody talks candidly to everybody as needed. Rank, function, or geographic distance does not distort communication and progress.

Besides simplifying its organization, GE has broken down walls that can isolate individuals. Boundarylessness has created a totally open and flexible corporate working environment. It allows meeting goals faster and more fully, both within and without. Learning and applying the best practices is another secret of GE's success, made possible by this corporate policy of boundarylessness that virtually eliminates "not-invented-here," while encouraging a high sense of responsibility among groups and individuals alike. This means that the disparate units of GE function seamlessly across businesses and geographic boundaries.

The implementation of boundarylessness was the stepping stone to large-scale offshore outsourcing. Once the idea of reaching out beyond corporate and geographic boundaries to improve processes was accepted, moving functions to offshore locations was just a step away. The cost, scale, and speed of service delivery from offshore locations discovered through the rigorous application of boundarylessness made the export of processes imperative.

GE's second principle of speed aims at faster turnaround times and shorter time-to-market. The speed of delivery is one of the key advantages of offshore delivery. Follow-the-sun development cycles, where software code is developed in different time zones, shortens project times substantially.

Stretch, the third principle, means going the extra mile to surpass set targets. With stretch, GE doubled its GDC target. This drove innovative approaches, which surpassed the target in half the time. Stretch goals are one of the key reasons for the quick ramp-up of offshore outsourcing to India. Offshore outsourcing fit perfectly with the strategies of boundarylessness, speed, and stretch.

A strong leader at the top drove the culture that made offshore outsourcing possible. "Boundaryless people, excited by speed and inspired by stretch dreams, have an absolutely infinite capacity to improve everything," Welch said.

By 1994, the concept of boundarylessness was broadcast throughout the organization and found place in GE annual report. The culture to send processes offshore was gaining acceptance in GE, and India was ready to handle the business. Says Bayman: "It was after Jack visited India once again in 1994 that the outsourcing process gathered steam. He witnessed the local talent, the GE culture and values being established in India and the corporate infrastructure being built. It was a natural for the company."

The imperative

GE decided to offshore processes for some compelling benefits: available intellectual talent, capacity, cost, speed to market, and ability to focus on core. In the IT space, like all other companies in the mid-1990s, GE faced a shortage of talent and the high cost of hiring software consultants in the US. India had a young population and a large educated workforce. Says Bayman: "Unlike other countries, India has long pipeline of talent making the cost benefit long term."

According to Guillermo Wille, JFWTC's managing director: "As far as the R&D center is concerned, the primary driver for setting up this team here is due to the intellectual talent pool available in India." The educational profile of the team at JFWTC (which includes technology teams from GE Global Research, GE Transportation Systems, GE Medical Systems, GE Power Systems, GE Plastics, and GE Aircraft Engines) consists of over 65 percent with advanced degrees, with about 20 percent of the total having PhDs.

Jeffery Immelt, CEO and chairman of GE, underscores the importance of the R&D center: "The most admired companies of the future will be known for their technical excellence. They will have the best products and services, powered by the best technology. In the GE of the 21st century, we will drive technical excellence in all our businesses and clearly distinguish ourselves in the marketplace. The Global Research Center is at the heart of this philosophy and will spearhead GE innovation and growth."

Even in the BPO space, cost and access to talent were prime reasons for going offshore. Says Bayman, "Going offshore and getting the required expertise locally was the only way to quickly grow. Our growth would have been much slower if processes were not moved to India." Another reason for moving processes offshore was the high attrition rate in US call centers, which is difficult and expensive to stem and could eventually affect the quality of processes. Welch says: "We can hire a level of talent in India for customer service and collection work that would be impossible to attract in the United States. Customer call centers in the United States are plagued by heavy turnover. In India these are sought-after jobs."

Says Bhasin: "In the case of BPO, the cost benefit offered by India has been a growth accelerator for GECIS." But customers that came for cost have stayed on for quality. GE brings down the roof on a function once it is outsourced to gain the full cost benefit. "Unless the operations on the customer site are fully shut down, the total cost savings will not be realized."

The availability of talent in India and lower costs are the strongest drivers to send processes offshore. GE saves about 25 percent of its costs on low-end call center jobs by moving them offshore. The cost-benefits of offshore outsourcing are expected to change in future due to currency fluctuations, rising productivity, falling telecom costs, and improving infrastructure.

In 1995, GE had strong reasons to ramp up its IT offshoring initiatives. Says Kocsi: "It was a strategic decision. GE's software outsourcing initiative hit a brick wall, so we looked for a way to change the game." Through centralization, GE brought the GDC's cost down. The suppliers did not have to bear marketing expenses for centers dedicated to a single customer. GE also extended its

173

telecommunications network directly to the supplier's site. The only expenses incurred by the supplier were facility and labor related, which are extremely low in India. Standardizing software development, maintenance, and conversion processes drove additional savings. "Offshoring forces you to define requirements up-front and follow structured change control, reducing scope creep and re-work."

The offshoring steps

Bayman, leading GE's Indian operations, was generally responsible for exporting processes offshore. In the US, CEOs of individual GE businesses, at the insistence of Welch, were pushing managers to export processes offshore to get benefit of cost, speed, and scale.

GE began outsourcing software development functions to India, followed by R&D and business processes. In 1994, the idea of sending accounting or contact center operations to a foreign land was unheard of. But offshoring software development was acceptable and necessary, as the US faced a shortage of software engineers and expensive IT development. Moving development to low-wage countries like India was essential to keep costs down and complete projects on time.

Bayman says: "There was resistance from some units to send software development offshore, but Jack just tightened budgets and the managers had to migrate development to overseas." The success of GE's offshore software development can be attributed to its leaders persistently driving the vision to actualization. Strong management commitment was needed initially to drive processes offshore. The management also had to deal with the pain of local layoffs.

Through a stringent selection process, GE appointed suppliers to execute software development processes offshore. It then set up GDCs in collaboration with suppliers, dedicated to developing software for GE. Following the offshore software development initiative, GE exported R&D tasks and then business processes.

Selling software outsourcing was much easier than selling BPO because the former was already going on when GE decided to offshore on a grand scale. And with the US shortage of IT people, offshore outsourcing served to bridge the talent gap cost-effectively. BPO was a different matter since talent shortage was not the critical issue. The key selling points were cost and the ability to concentrate on core, and this took a lot of internal selling. The BPO selling process began in 1998; by 2001, the concept had caught on, and GECIS was running at full capacity.

Says Bayman: "One of the initial problems with BPO was that GE units in the US treated GECIS like a vendor and that had to be changed to make the working relationship more effective." GE then tightly integrated its Indian operation with that of the US in software outsourcing, BPO, and R&D outsourcing. The GE units in the US took ownership of the processes running in India, which meant that a GE Medical call center run by GECIS would report to a GE Medical manager in the US and also the GECIS manager in India. GECIS pays salaries and bonuses and evaluates and promotes employees. "The operations are truly seamless now and the Indian leader reports to the US leader."

The JFWTC is GE's first and largest R&D center outside the US. An integral part of GE Global Research, the center is integrated with its counterparts in the US. The leadership for a research team is selected based on the location where the expertise lies. Centers of Excellence (COEs) are set up according to the talent pool available in their location, so it is not necessary that all R&D projects be led by the US operations in GE's Global Research organization. The projects are mapped to enable global teams to report to their leaders, wherever they may be based. After the success of the JFWTC in India, similar centers have been set up in China and Germany.

According to Wille: "R&D activities (including fundamental research) are divided into a portfolio of projects that span various timelines in terms of their impact on the business. Ready-to-serve (RTS) projects constitute 10 percent of the center's R&D programs and are short term with an immediate impact and technical challenges; the multi-generation product plans (MGPPs) take products and services to the next evolution and these typically impact the business in one to three years."

The COEs work on technologies that JFWTC and business leaders decide will make a significant impact on the marketplace in the next three to five years if the technical challenges are resolved. "The MGPP and COE programs constitute about 70 percent of the activities undertaken at GE Global Research while the advanced technology programs (ATPs) which are five to ten years out would change the game for a business, or create a whole new market, if they come to fruition. These would constitute about a 20 percent of our programs," says Wille. The JFWTC's increased focus on ATPs at GE Global Research also includes such areas as nanotechnology, biotechnology, light energy conversion, photonics, advanced propulsion and hydrogen energy.

GE exports processes to either wholly owned operations or suppliers, depending on how critical they are. All offshore centers are tightly integrated with the operations in the US, and the GE customer is always the owner of the process, even if a supplier runs the center. Says Bayman: "GE takes the wholly owned route to gain productivity like in the case of GECIS or to keep intellectual property in-house which is also the rationale to have the technology center run by GE." Outsourcing gives GE both cost and productivity benefits. To ensure quality at supplier-run software development centers, GE requires that people working on the project be at least Six Sigma green belt certified and that the vendor have some black belts and master black belts.

Exporting business processes to India was Bhasin's idea. The capital businesses in India were not making any impact on GE globally, and moving into BPO would make that happen. The scope of BPO in GE was so large that the initiative was bound to create ripples in all of GE's global operations. Bhasin went with the idea to Nigel Andrews, senior president of GE Capital's global operations. Initially, both Bhasin and Bayman had to do a lot of internal selling. After a few success stories, Welch began showcasing the successes at leadership meets. Now, processes move almost automatically to India. With the success of BPO in India, GE has expanded to China and Mexico and plans to enter Hungary to serve the non-English-speaking nations in Europe.

BPO offshoring

Initially, GECIS, the Indian BPO unit of GE, studied American Express's and British Airways' successful BPO operations in India. It even hired Raman Roy, head of American Express's BPO operations, to set up and run GE's initiative. GECIS pulled together a strong local team, most of them from GE, where the capital business was not doing well and many top performers were being underutilized.

Roy set up the first call center in a business environment where permission for telecom lines was difficult to obtain from the government. Once dedicated lines were available, GECIS was set to go. GECIS commenced operations in the mail space, making address changes and making calls into the US for credit card collections.

Once the operations reached a critical mass, GECIS needed a selling strategy and roped in champions to push the initiative. Bhasin says: "We decided to target non-core activities and told potential customers to come for cost and stay for quality. And to deliver the promise we ensured that our processes were flawless and overwhelmed the centers with resources. We also told our GE customers that their back-end processes were core functions for us." The economic proposition of coming to India was convincing. The cost of labor was substantially lower, and once GECIS got the order, it was executed faultlessly.

GECIS had the strongest champions in then-president of GE Capital, Gary Wendt, and in Jack Welch, Scott Bayman, and Pramod Bhasin. Bayman met Welch a couple of times to sell the BPO idea. After a few successes, Welch and Wendt asked the managers of GE units to visit India and see the center. Both Bhasin and Bayman used their contacts in the US to sell the services of GECIS. Once Welch and Wendt began selling the concept at annual conferences, getting new business was much easier.

Along with the selling, GECIS was strengthening its sales and delivery mechanisms. GECIS sent about 15 to 20 relationship managers to the US to interact with the customer on a daily basis. Working closely with the customer, these managers would also identify processes to be shipped offshore. Once the processes were identified, a solution identification and migration team would fly to the US to ship the process back. If the process had flaws, it would be fixed on-site or offshore, depending on the situation.

The delivery arm of GECIS was expanded to meet the increasing demand. Says Bhasin: "We were able to find very good talent locally." In India, GECIS hired graduates: Its first advertisement elicited 8,000 responses. "Seeing the responses, we realized that we were on the edge of something big." As the delivery centers in

India expanded, GECIS began taking over more complex functions.

The operations side faced challenges due to regulations and to a lack of back-up facilities for power and telecom. There were logistical issues of working at night to serve the US markets, as there is about a 12-hour time difference between the two countries. Also, when making outgoing calls, call center representatives lacked the contextual knowledge that was very necessary to making a sale. Says Bhasin: "In the initial phases we learnt a lot through trial and error." To give call center representatives the contextual knowledge, GECIS and the customer created specialized training programs. To get the requisite telecom and power back-up, GE worked with the regulatory authorities. To solve the logistics problem to getting people to work at night, GE provided transportation to employees.

There was a huge demand for data entry from GE units, a service provided out of Mexico. Delivering this service from India did not make sense, as the telecom costs were 10 times as high.

GECIS moved up the value chain by offering services closer to the core functions of their customers. To get the required expertise in accounts and analytics, GECIS flew talent from the US to India. To build world-class management and attain the capabilities of US counterparts, GECIS often sends talent to the US to gain expertise to run centers in India.

The analytics COE based in Bangalore provides modeling and analytics support to GE Capital businesses to improve their processes and profitability. The center provides data-driven business strategies to such functional areas as asset management, collections, fraud detection, marketing, pricing, and risk management. Says Bhasin: "We are constantly moving up the value chain and the bulk of the growth will be up in the chain in areas like e-learning, analytics, and so on."

The relationship between GECIS and its GE customers is really a partnership. The customer continues to own the processes run by GECIS, and the GECIS manager also reports to the client. "The customer is a hands-on manager," says Bhasin. The customer, in fact, treats the operations run in GECIS as just another department, and the processes are replicated to run as if they were operated on-site.

GECIS also provides surge resources to its customers to smooth the peaks and valleys in demand. These can be used, for instance, to integrate companies or portfolios acquired by GE, which happen more at random than at specific times, making it is impossible for a business to optimally allocate resources to the integration functions continuously.

As GECIS established its success, Bhasin has taken it to new levels of efficiency. He has formed Global GECIS to leverage intellectual talent into Europe and South Africa. "The goal is to balance cost and get the best talent anywhere in the globe." Bhasin has also institutionalized all BPO practices to gain both business and process expertise.

As processes were being outsourced, GE had to deal with the loss of jobs locally. Its culture took care of that aspect to a large extent. Says Bhasin: "GE has a culture of aggressive cost cutting and productivity to stay profitable." Although GECIS exported nearly 11,000 jobs, GE in the US did not lose this number of employees. In some cases, people were redeployed into other areas or started performing services that had been done for GE by outside vendors in the US. In fact, the first processes to be exported were those run by GE vendors in the US: This minimized the impact on GE employees. In areas like analytics, GECIS supplemented services delivered in the US by adding jobs in India.

Software outsourcing

GE divided IT into three segments: business process re-engineering, product software, and commodity support. It decided to retain all the business process re-engineering on-site; send product software, which required high investments in human intellectual capital, to GE-owned software centers; and send commodity support to the GDCs. "Then we used the 70:70:70 rule to measure each business unit's progress," adds Kocsi—70 percent of IT effort outsourced, 70 percent of outsourced effort to a GDC, and 70 percent of GDC work performed offshore. "The metric added clarity, ensuring everyone understood the deliverable."

Kocsi, who was responsible for exporting software development and maintenance processes to GDCs in India, adds: "GE adopted the sheltering strategy used by many manufacturing firms." This means that GE owns the intellectual property, but the dedicated staff and facilities are not on GE's balance sheet. The supplier

179

incurs the expenses of running the offshore development center, and GE pays only for services it uses. As well, the vendors are included in GE's IT networks to create virtual co-locations, work spaces that are connected through an IT network with similar operating processes, providing the same look and feel.

GE decided to not own the GDCs since they were cost centers and did not generate external (non-GE) revenue. Says Kocsi: "If software is the product's secret sauce, GE should own it. Anybody can build CAT scanners, but the algorithms that generate the images are proprietary to GE." The criterion used to decide between owning versus sheltering was intellectual property: If the product or process is GE proprietary, GE owns the offshore center running it. For example, GE owns the JFWTC but not offshore centers working on an Oracle project.

Before outsourcing, GE categorized and inventoried all the software applications that could be exported. Says Kocsi: "India was a no-brainer. The country had more English-speaking IT graduates than the next 10 countries combined, including the US." After India began its economic liberalization and the rupee was allowed to float freely against other currencies, Indian currency began to depreciate. GE saw a long-term value coming to India, given the favorable trend in exchange rates.

GE executives flew to India and set up shop at a Bangalore hotel and invited top Indian IT companies to pitch for the business. To be qualified for the GDC selection process, potential suppliers needed a minimum size of 1,500 people because GE did not want vendors to earn more than one-third of their income from GE. GE selected three vendors—Patni Computer Services, Wipro Infotech, and Tata Consultancy Services (TCS)—to set up GDCs. It was a strict selection process with several incumbent suppliers like Infosys eliminated. TCS and Patni built GDCs in Mumbai, and Wipro in Bangalore. Under the sheltering strategy, the vendors ran the GDCs on GE's network within the firewalls.

Running the GDCs at an optimum level was crucial to the success of the offshoring initiative. Since vendors invest heavily upfront, it was important that they get adequate returns. "The trick was to run the centers at a high utilization rate," says Kocsi. Therefore, the centers needed about 400 to 500 people at the site to achieve economies of scale. The centers also had dedicated hardware people and were to run rigid quality metrics. "We have rejected a lot of proposals. Projects with well-defined requirements and high offshore content tend to be the most successful." Kocsi would also sit with every GE business to see what should be outsourced and help decide which GDC would get the project. His gatekeeping allowed GE to control capacity and ensured optimum utilization. As outsourcing ramped up, GE began applying the 70:70:70 principle to the process.

To ensure that the GDCs were functioning optimally, GE project managers measured them every quarter on communications, uptime, and other quantitative and qualitative metrics. Their visits also ensured that GE had a tight control on the GDCs and GE's quality processes were strictly adhered to.

GE concentrated on developing skills at the GDCs through hiring and training to ensure that their resources were at the cutting edge of technology. To keep costs low, GE worked with the GDCs to forecast staffing requirements and avoid over-capacity.

GE dedicated GDCs' staff to individual businesses to enable the centers to obtain domain expertise. It also made reporting relationships simpler. "Having the infrastructure and facilities in place enabled change acceleration," says Kocsi.

One factor in the success of the GDC model was GE's strict quality and cost model, enforced by GE's process controls. The initial stages of strong control ensured suppliers absorbed GE's culture and methodologies. Once the processes stabilized at the GDC, the control was relaxed.

GDCs in their final form were a virtual extension of GE's information management support. They had exclusive resources catering to specific GE units and were organized by domain expertise, not technology. They had high utilization rates and understood the client's environments. The GDCs institutionalized quality and productivity measurements. The GDC also brought intellectual property protection and secured operations, people and facilities at a reduced cost, and management and training.

Exported processes

GE Capital in India offers offshore outsourcing services to GE and to strategic customers worldwide. By outsourcing non-core processes, it enables its businesses to focus resources on key aspects of their operations.

GE units outsource transaction processing, accounting, and call center operations to GECIS, the BPO arm of GE India. GE Software Solutions provides services in the technology domains of Oracle applications, Siebel, Shana, and Vision Plus, including implementation, development, transition, maintenance and support, and upgrades. The team operates from state-of-the-art offshore centers in Hyderabad and Gurgaon.

GE Capital Integrated Business Solutions builds global business platforms, IT-enabled services, and product-specific solutions for its global customers.

IProcess, a joint venture of GE Capital and Mastech, a software company with centers in India, provides a range of IT-enabled BPO services such as helpdesk and e-commerce fulfillment with Web-based customer service. GE outsources key initiatives in IT to the five vendors—Birlasoft, Mascot Systems, Patni, Satyam Computer Services, and TCS—which run the GDCs.

Analytics COE provides modeling and analytics support to GE Capital businesses worldwide to improve their processes and profitability in such functional areas as asset management, collections, fraud, marketing, pricing, and risk.

GE conducts R&D at the JFWTC, an integrated multidisciplinary facility, where scientists, researchers, and engineers work jointly with their US counterparts in electromagnetic analytics, engineering analysis, computational fluid dynamics, composite material design, color technology, additive technology, non-destructive evaluation, corrosion technology, MEMS, molecular modeling, power electronics, and analysis technologies.

The Advanced Mechanical Technologies (AMT) team gives a technological edge to GE businesses in mechanical systems design, acoustics, material modeling and new applications development, x-ray sources and systems, reliability, and mechanical transmission systems, including gears and bearings. The lab is equipped with bearing test rigs, facilities for thermoforming and weatherability studies, acoustic/noise testing, and high-precision testing equipment for appliance performance. The AMT team has filed over 60 patent disclosures.

The Chemical Engineering and Modeling Lab are integral to GE Plastics' business plans. The lab focuses on process engineering, process modeling, and process development for a variety of chemical industries like petrochemicals, specialty chemicals, engineering industries, and polymers worldwide.

The Chemistry and Catalysis team converts fundamental chemistry into applications in such areas as monomers, color technology, additives, stabilizers, and FRs, using enablers like molecular modeling, synthesis, catalysis (green chemistry), analytical solutions, product stewardship, process technology, and sourcing. The team is researching new chemical entities and finding ways of manufacturing them. It develops eco-friendly yet cost-efficient processes at its COEs in molecular modeling, color chemistry, separation techniques, NMR, trace level analysis, and PBT profiling. The team works for GE Plastics and GE Specialty Materials.

The Electronic and Photonic Systems Technologies (EPST) team works in the technology areas of electric power, electromechanical system control, and specialty electrical technologies. It applies its expertise in such areas as power electronics, power systems, controls, electronics reliability, electrical insulation, and electromagnetics to focus on achieving cutting-edge results in industrial electronic systems, transportation, and water technologies. The ESPT team has developed such technologies as hybrid vehicles, improved efficiency of electrical machines, and advanced controls for turbines. It has improved product performance and generated a better understanding of electrical systems for GE businesses like GE Industrial Systems, GE Transportation Systems, GE Power Systems, and GE Medical Systems in turbine controls, motor controls, and distributed generation.

The Global Energy and Propulsion Technology lab (EPTL) focuses on technology for aircraft engines, power turbines, generators, diesel engines, and appliances, with research and development in combustion energy systems, fluid mechanics, prognostics, propulsion, and thermal systems. Part of the global EPTL team is the Engine Analysis and Prognostics lab (EAPL), the hub of concentrated research in computational fluid dynamics and remote monitoring and diagnostics. The EAPL team works on various short- and long-term projects for GE Transportation Systems, GE Power Systems, GE Aircraft Engines, GE Specialty Materials, and GE Appliances. The EPTL has the well-defined COEs for applied computational fluid dynamics (CFD) and real-time prognostics. The former is involved in modeling, design and performance analysis for products to suggest improvements in efficiency and elegance of operations through its in-house expertise in CFD, including cold flow analysis and combustion; the latter focuses on real-time performance forecast and anomaly detection to reduce downtime of such equipment as gas turbines and steam turbines.

The Materials Research team works in advanced ceramics and metallurgy. The multi-disciplinary team, consisting of material scientists, metallurgists, physicists, chemists, and chemical engineers, studies synthesis of novel materials, process development, advanced characterization techniques, testing, simulation, and modeling as well as new product development. The team has contributed significantly in the development of high-permeability materials, high-efficiency phosphors, and synthesis of nano powders. It has ongoing research programs affecting the various GE businesses through COEs for powder synthesis and process development, corrosion, structure-property modeling, and tribology.

The Micro and Nano Structures Technologies (MNST) team works in electronics design, device modeling, and electronics materials development. Electronics sub-system design includes circuit and integrated circuit (ASIC) design and simulation. It does work for GE Industrial Systems, GE Medical Systems, GE Transportation Systems, GE Specialty Materials, and GE Consumer Products. The Device Modeling group works on modeling and designing MEMS based sensors, wide-band gap semiconductor devices, optical properties of the materials, and quantum chemistry modeling for organic light emitting diodes for a wide range of applications.

The Electronic Materials Development group's activities include application-specific formulation of polymer-based materials for electronic packaging, thin-film characterization (organic and inorganic), and moisture and oxygen permeability testing for barrier coatings.

The Polymers and Synthetic Materials (PSM) lab, part of the GE Plastics technology team, works in polymer design and synthesis, structure-property correlations, polymer composites, and polymer processing and advanced polymer characterization studies. The team focuses on designing and developing cost-effective polymeric materials for advanced applications and producing better materials for automotive, optical media, telecom, and electrical and electronic applications. Its lab has established COEs for electron microscopy, filler technology, emulsion polymers, UL agency testing, and engineering data generation.

The Power Systems Technologies (PST) team develops state-of-the-art IT solutions to re-engineer and Web-enable engineering and business processes. It establishes processes for improving productivity in GE Businesses, integrates disparate data systems, creates toolkits and wizards for data management and analysis, and provides a framework to manage resources (people, facilities, and documents) over the Internet. The team has filed for patents in Web-based action item tracking and Web-based automatic inspection form generation. The PST lab is the COE for e-engineering.

The Information and Decision Technologies (IDT) team works in predictive reliability and modeling, time series forecasting, econometrics, risk analytics, quantitative finance, predictive biology, biostatistics prediction, fusion technologies, machine learning, probabilistic text mining, pattern recognition, data visualization techniques, and data mining. The Prediction Algorithms COE focuses on prediction algorithms to drive a shift from a reactive diagnosis mode to a proactive predictive prognosis mode. The IDT COE works with GE Consumer Finance, GE Medical Systems (GEMS), GE Industrial Systems (GEIS), and GE Power Systems (GEPS) businesses.

The Imaging Technologies (ImT) team works in virtual imaging, clinical visualization, and image communications, where it has contributed in the areas of bone segmentation for unobstructed viewing of blood vessels, beam-former design for superior image quality for ultrasound, TruRez image codec for high-end PACS, breast lesion characterization in ultrasound, motion/object detection and tracking algorithms, model for lung nodules, scatter correction for abdominal phantom images, x-ray image registration and fused visualization for 3D roadmap, CT detector optimization, optimum algorithms for modeling the CT scanner, Bloch simulator, pulse simulator and artifact simulators for the MRI, and algorithmic acceleration of image delivery in PET.

The Clinical Visualization team develops tools to enhance the productivity and accuracy of the clinician (radiologist, surgeon, or referring physician) during diagnosis, prognosis, and therapy. These tools automate selective enhancement of image features to emphasize the relevant anatomical and physiological information.

The Image Communication group works on progressive multi-resolution-based image codecs that affect the diagnostic workflow of hospitals. The faster codecs improve radiologists' productivity; compression ratio helps to optimize storage needs and reduces transmission time over networks. The group also focuses on novel schemes for embedded applications and medical data retrieval.

The Industrial Imaging and Modeling Lab (IIML) conducts advanced research in imaging, image processing, image archival, geometry modeling, and physics modeling aimed at providing technology solutions for industrial inspection and manufacturing. It drives the development and standardization of imaging platforms for analyzing inspection data, integration of geometry and image data for enhanced visualization and decision support, analysis of new inspection probe designs through physics based modeling, and digitization of the manufacturing process through a unique combination of real-time inspection and image processing, process modeling, and numerical control. The IIML team focuses on the needs of GE Aircraft Engines, GE Power Systems, and GE Specialty Materials.

Benefits

GE achieved tremendous benefits from the offshoring exercise in terms of cost, speed, quality, focus on core, and access to top-notch talent. Welch remarks: "India has a wealth of highly educated people who can do many different things very well. GE Capital moved its customer service centers to Delhi, and the results have been sensational. Our Indian global customer centers have had better quality, lower costs, better collection rates, and greater customer acceptance than our comparable operations in the United States and Europe."

Annualized cost savings are expected to reach $1 billion by 2005. Processes in the lower end of the value chain have offered savings of almost 25 percent and those in the high end as much as 60 percent. For instance, in a call center, the cost per employee in India works out to $18,000 to $25,000 a year, including compensation and benefits plus overhead costs; in the US, it would be $40,000. A CPA would cost $80,000 a year in the US versus $30,000 in India. As telecom expenses, which now constitute 18 percent of the costs, fall and GE moves to less expensive locations in the smaller cities of India, the costs are expected to further drop.

Says Bayman: "Moving non-core processes enabled GE to concentrate and grow in the core areas of business. Without the offshore outsourcing initiative, growth could have stymied." Bhasin states that the GE's Analytics Center in India enabled its GE units to enter new markets by providing them with better data on customers. The center has also performed pricing analysis that helped the GE units get more customers by giving them the right price.

GECIS has set up IT helpdesks in India to assist GE employees worldwide with day-to-day issues. This has freed the IT resources on the customer site to build better software systems for the company. India also provides surge resources to GE units worldwide, used to integrate companies or portfolios into the GE system after an acquisition. To provide these resources from the customer's pool would be expensive and take the focus of the acquisition teams away from acquiring assets to integrating them.

Surge resources are also available to other GE functions and can be ramped up or down, as the customer needs. This gives the customer a better ability to quote prices in the marketplace. There have also been quality improvements in the processes sent offshore. Says Bhasin: "In 90 percent of the processes, we have made considerable quality improvements." In some cases, processes exported to India have been taken to the Sigma 5 levels from Sigma 2 or 3. "We assist our customers to get to the net income goals."

The non-core processes exported to India get the management time and attention of core functions since back-end operations for the customer are front functions for the offshore center.

In the software space, GE's GDC model reduced software costs substantially and provided access to a stable pool of IT talent that was difficult to get in the US. The GDC model also ensured that GE retained control over the operations of the offshore centers and could continuously bring down costs through process improvements.

In the R&D space, GE has access to one of the best talent pools in the world, which has led to several technology breakthroughs at the JFWTC. As the section on R&D processes exported by GE discusses, individual teams have contributed extensively to GE businesses worldwide.

Conclusion

The GE experience shows that offshore outsourcing not only is possible but also brings great cost and quality benefits. Bayman, Bhasin, and Kocsi feel that companies should aggressively look at offshore outsourcing, as the economics are very compelling. If companies have any doubt, they should go visit the offshore centers and see first-hand the energy and benefits provided.

Before going offshore, companies must decide between insourcing and outsourcing. Says Bayman: "If you decide to do it yourself, get a champion in the US and a strong networked guy in India to run the operations." This is important to sell the concept to internal clients in the US. An Indian operations person networked in the US will be able to carry the relationship forward and smooth rough edges in the relationship.

It is best to start the outsourcing initiative small and increase the scope after a few successes. Publicizing successes will promote quick acceptance of the offshore outsourcing concept within the organization. "Finally to make an impact and get a high degree of benefits, outsource a critical mass," says Bayman. As more processes are exported, the original owners in the US or Europe might lose interest. "Always ensure that the process is owned by the customer." This ensures that vendor initiates process and quality improvements consistent with the objectives of the customer.

Keeping a back-up plan is always important. The customer should identify which functions are critical and ensure that the vendor puts up disaster recovery sites for them to get the process running if one site goes down. Says Bhasin: "A business continuity plan is important." The critical processes should be mapped to move back to either the customer or a different center in case of an emergency.

The Northwestern Mutual Story

Northwestern Mutual is a Fortune 500 mutual life insurance company with premium revenues of $10.1 billion and net investment income of $5.5 billion. In a mutual insurance company, a participating policy's ultimate value depends on the dividends paid to policy owners, which reflect the company's underlying investment returns, insurance benefits, and expenses: Dividends for 2003 are expected to be a record $3.8 billion. Superior product value contributes to policy owners' satisfaction and loyalty. In 2002, they elected to use more than 75 percent of their 2002 dividends to purchase additional insurance protection, helping increase total life insurance in force to $750 billion.

A mutual life insurance company's surplus provides the organization and its policy owners with protection against the unexpected, while an asset valuation reserve (AVR) supports a long-term investment strategy by cushioning against short-term market volatility. At year end 2002, total surplus and AVR of $8.5 billion represented 11.4 percent of general account insurance reserves. Northwestern Mutual's current level of financial strength compares favorably with its historical levels and helps assure the company's promise of financial security for policy owners.

Genesis

Matching the financial strength and security of Northwestern Mutual is its commitment to leverage technology to speed business processes. The company's first system was a 20K IBM 705, a state-of-the-art machine in 1957, the first step in a ground-breaking strategy that Northwestern Mutual continues to follow today: Maximize service and performance through the use of the most advanced computer technology available. It was inevitable that the company would begin to tap offshore resources to bridge the shortage of available talent that the US faced in the mid-1990s. Northwestern Mutual's financial strength could have made hiring resources locally possible, but the need to get the right resources at the right time prompted the company to look offshore.

Northwestern Mutual regularly updates its tools and adopts new technologies. Its current multi-platform environment integrates IBM-compatible mainframes, servers, personal computers, personal digital assistants, and other computing appliances.

Northwestern Mutual went online with LINK (Life Information Network) in 1976 to connect all remote sales offices with the home office computer system and databases in Milwaukee, Wisconsin. Later, other constituents of the company were added to the network. With the growing adoption of client server computing, the environment changed: In addition to mainframes and servers, the number of personal computers grew to more than 10,000 in the home office and field sales offices. Work groups at the home office were interconnected through LANs and given access to a variety of Windows-based productivity tools, packaged solutions, and systems written in-house.

With the rapid development of the Internet, Northwestern Mutual implemented a Web-based architecture for its distribution system. It developed NMFN.com, a Web site for its Northwestern Mutual Financial Network, and MutualNet, the company's corporate intranet. It also has LinkNet, an intranet for its field force, as well as other advanced Web-based capabilities.

The company's information systems department works to identify, evaluate, select, and deploy the most effective and responsive solutions to business issues that require the use of systems and technology resources: It delivers solutions through internal or external (offshore or on-site vendors) resources; maintains and operates hardware and software systems to meet negotiated business service levels; and makes decisions on an enterprise basis, leveraging technology investments across business units and products.

To efficiently run all its transactions, database requests, reports, online responses, and other tasks, the information systems department of Northwestern Mutual has more than 700 employees in these primary functional areas:

- Systems and programming plans, develops, and enhances business systems, data administration, training, and client computing. It supports sales, marketing, underwriting, billing and collection, investments, accounting, and claims.

- Technology services is responsible for developing and maintaining systems software, tuning computer environments, running database management systems, co-ordinating the development of architectures, evaluating and recommending new equipment, consulting, training, WAN and LAN planning, telecommunications, and some enterprise-wide applications such as e-mail.

- The operations unit is responsible for running the Computer Center. Operating 24/7, it has a helpdesk that supports both home office and sales office clients. The focus on architecture enables researching, recommending, acquiring, and communicating systems-architecture standards and guidelines for the purpose of developing, revising, and communicating strategies and directions for Northwestern Mutual's information technologies.

The emphasis and dependence of Northwestern Mutual's processes on technology made it susceptible to the IT resource shortage in the US as a result of the Y2K bug. Says Walt Wojcik, former CIO of the company: "With the challenge of Y2K, a lot of code had to be examined, and, if necessary, changed. Moreover, the company had several new business initiatives that required IT support. To address the issues, we adopted a flexible staffing model and began the analysis and search for the supporting resources."

Wojcik believes that all competitive advantage is temporary in today's rapidly changing marketplace. To address the challenge, he suggests that IT systems and processes be flexible and responsive. This led to Northwestern Mutual's first tentative steps in offshore outsourcing as part of its staffing model, described as selective sourcing.

Why

In the late 1990s, the economy was booming, and IT resources throughout North America were in short supply and expensive. Northwestern Mutual saw an opportunity to grow; however, the shortage of resources to support its initiatives was a potential threat. The company's needs were two-fold: to supplement its talented staff with sufficient new resources to capture new business opportunities, and to stay on the cutting-edge of technology.

"Given the rapid changes in technology and our surge in demand for IT personnel, we adopted a flexible staffing model," says Wojcik. "We needed to get the right resources at the right time and cost-effectively. Whatever the source of external supplemental resources, however, we wanted to be certain that

Northwestern Mutual's experienced staff would be used to focus on new opportunities." Given the supply and demand imbalances at the time, it was apparent that all its needs could not be met through US resources alone. "We needed foreign partners with access to IT talent to satisfy our requirements."

Wojcik also felt that with the changing technology environment, there was less need to build proprietary applications as Northwestern Mutual had in the past. "Our strategy dictated that we build systems for competitive advantage but buy for competitive parity."

How

To address Y2K and to stay competitive in the marketplace, Northwestern Mutual had to secure supplemental resources. It needed the IT infrastructure to be in place to launch new products quickly when the market demanded it. Say Wojcik: "Since sourcing in North America was proving to be difficult we looked outside the US." Before being the CIO, Wojcik had served several roles on the business side, including both senior VP of planning and CFO; this made him a very powerful ambassador to drive a new sourcing model that included offshore resources.

To begin outsourcing, Wojcik looked for a country that had IT talent, was politically stable, had English language and communication skills, and was on the other side of the world to better use the company's available computer hardware and take advantage of the 24/7 software development concept. "India was the obvious choice." Northwestern Mutual also looked for a partner that best matched its own reputation as "the most respected life insurance company," according to *Fortune* magazine. Moreover, it wanted a company with a similar commitment to quality; as a result, it chose Infosys Technologies.

As the outsourcing exercise began, the message was sent throughout the organization that IT strategy was not just about IT systems but client processes as well. Hence, the offshoring initiative involved all departments whose processes were affected. Once there was a buy-in from the respective department, the ramp-up was rapid. "The initiative had a slow beginning, but from 1995 to 2000, we kept doubling offshoring resources each year." Moreover, the nature of the processes outsourced grew beyond simply Y2K support to a variety of both tactical and strategic applications.

To ensure a smooth relationship, Northwestern Mutual facilitated a cultural exchange meeting, which consisted of equal proportions of employees of both companies. Its goal was to promote an understanding of behaviors, mannerisms, accents, and cultures. The exchange found that the two companies had a lot more in common, such as focus on work and family, which served to strengthen the relationship over time. To move work offshore rapidly, Infosys and Northwestern Mutual exchanged managers, moving them between the US and India. Both companies selected one high-level relationship manager to manage the exchange.

Once the offshoring exercise began, Northwestern Mutual concluded that an offshore component model consisting of 80 percent of the IT resources based in India and 20 percent on-site would provide the best model for good communication and competitive pricing. The company had three other vendors locally, with one using offshore H1B visa resources, to ensure leverage with growth. However, according to Wojcik: "Infosys is our largest vendor and our relationship with them is still very strong."

Before selecting a vendor, Northwestern Mutual had no presence in Asia except as an investor. Through the support of its investment department, Northwestern Mutual's IT department was able to gather extremely valuable information about the financial strength, management, and culture of several IT service vendors.

Early in the selection process, others had offered to provide Northwestern Mutual offshore services. However, since these companies were based in the US, with smaller development centers in Asia, their North American overheads pushed up prices substantially.

What was offshored

Initially, Northwestern Mutual used offshore resources exclusively for Y2K programming. Says Wojcik: "Coupled with the expense savings and bolstered by the quality of the work product, the expanded use of the model for several additional applications was inevitable. Both tactical and strategic work was increasingly outsourced." However, concerned about security and customer privacy, the company kept the application support work on-site.

Northwestern Mutual had invested in encrypting data and was considering additional investments in masking technologies to make online transactions even more secure.

The company has not outsourced any corporate or other business processes and may not do so in the near future. It has very low overhead and operating costs and sees no immediate reason to send processes offshore. "Northwestern Mutual enjoys a very low ratio of operations cost to premium collected and that limits the immediate need to consider process outsourcing. We have a 35 to 40 percent advantage over competition."

Benefits

"We received tremendous benefits in the areas of cost and timely access to IT talent by going offshore. Moreover, we were able to focus our internal resources on our core activities in pursuit of competitive advantage," says Wojcik. With cost benefit due to the labor arbitrage and India's pool of IT talent, availability of quality resources was never a problem. Once several non-core IT tasks were sent offshore, the IT department was able to concentrate on building systems to enable new product launches. "With offshoring giving us the ability to focus on the most significant business opportunities, we were able to rapidly launch several new products such as variable universal life insurance."

At Northwestern Mutual, the IT budget is 25 to 30 percent of the company's operational budget. "Even though the absolute expenses on IT have increased, we got a lot more for our dollar by going offshore." Another benefit was in process improvement. Infosys has excellent processes for IT development and maintenance and has been assessed by SEI as one of the top software companies in process maturity. Several processes at Infosys were shared with the company and adopted in the US providing productivity benefits. "We learned a lot of good processes from Infosys and so enjoyed additional benefits and values apart from low cost."

Index

About the Author

Dr. Nandu Thondavadi is an Adjunct Professor of Management at the Kellogg School of Management, Northwestern University and the founding Managing Director of Mascon Global Limited, an offshore software services company. Nandu brings his exceptional academic and real life learning to bear in authoring this book.

George Albert is the managing editor of www.capturetrends.com and a freelance business journalist authoring articles in the areas of management strategy, technology, finance and economy. He brought his extensive research, writing, and interviewing skills in the creation of this book.

Preface by Scott Bayman

Scott Bayman is a pioneer in the offshore outsourcing space. As corporate officer of the General Electric Company and President and Chief Executive Officer of GE India, he has overseen the successful migration of diverse software, research & development, and business processes to India.

Mr. Bayman was closely involved with this book project and wrote its preface, leveraging years of offshore outsourcing experience. His initiatives are projected to save GE nearly $ 1 billion each year by 2005. Mr. Bayman joined GE in 1987 and assumed his present position in 1993, after relocating to India.

Printed in the United States
56441LVS00003B/151-156